REFERENCE AND EXISTENCE

REFERENCE AND EXISTENCE

The John Locke Lectures

Saul A. Kripke

OXFORD
UNIVERSITY PRESS

OXFORD

UNIVERSITY PRESS

Oxford University Press is a department of the University of Oxford.
It furthers the University's objective of excellence in research,
scholarship, and education by publishing worldwide.

Oxford   New York
Auckland   Cape Town   Dar es Salaam   Hong Kong   Karachi
Kuala Lumpur   Madrid   Melbourne   Mexico City   Nairobi
New Delhi   Shanghai   Taipei   Toronto

With offices in
Argentina   Austria   Brazil   Chile   Czech Republic   France   Greece
Guatemala   Hungary   Italy   Japan   Poland   Portugal   Singapore
South Korea   Switzerland   Thailand   Turkey   Ukraine   Vietnam

Oxford is a registered trade mark of Oxford University Press
in the UK and certain other countries.

Published in the United States of America by
Oxford University Press
198 Madison Avenue, New York, NY 10016

Library of Congress Cataloging-in-Publication Data
Kripke, Saul A., 1940–
Reference and existence : the John Locke lectures / Saul A. Kripke.
pages cm.
Includes bibliographical references (pages   ) and index.
ISBN 978-0-19-992838-5 (hardcover : alk. paper)
1. Reference (Philosophy) 2. Ontology. I. Title.
B105.R25K75   2013
121'.68—dc23   2012038713

1006986136

3 5 7 9 8 6 4 2

Printed in the United States of America
on acid-free paper

To
My Father

CONTENTS

PREFACE

Some time ago I found myself browsing through Moore's *Some Main Problems of Philosophy*, looking for a passage I wished to quote. The passage was not there, but I came across the following: "I hope Professor Wisdom was right in thinking that this book was worth publishing. It consists of twenty lectures which I delivered at Morley College in London in the winter of 1910–11." The book, however, was only published in 1953.

I must admit the finding cheered me up a bit, since I was myself in a similar situation, trying to prepare for publication a set of lectures I had delivered in 1973 as the John Locke Lectures at Oxford, and wondering whether publication would still be of some interest. My lectures were entitled "Reference and Existence," and the fact that they have now become the book you are reading (I was going to say, "the book you have in your hands," but who knows if that is true anymore?) indicates that, with some trepidation, I have finally published my John Locke Lectures.

There are difficult decisions that need to be made when preparing for publication material written (or spoken!) long before. I have tried to adopt a fairly conservative attitude toward the original lectures, intervening only when, it seemed to me now, it was needed. Although I have added most of the footnotes, replaced passages that could use clarification, compressed some that now seemed too long (or difficult to comprehend), and even extended some that seemed too short, I can say that the final text remains faithful to the lectures as they were delivered. This is so even though the view of negative existentials stated at the end was highly complicated and one that I was not wholly satisfied with, even at the time, nor yet today. But it is not as though, at present, I am wholly satisfied with or prefer *any* alternative.

Probably the most substantial contribution of the lectures was the ontology of fictional and mythical characters, conceived of as abstract objects whose existence depends on the existence or non-existence of various fictional or mythological works. I took natural language as my guide, which just quantifies over these things. Thus, I did not intend to apply the notion to 'Vulcan,' 'phlogiston,' or other vacuous theoretical names of a more recent vintage, which are 'mythological' objects only in a highly extended and perhaps even metaphorical sense of 'mythological.' However, I am not entirely sure of the difference in principle between such erroneously postulated scientific entities and the figures of myth (which were, after all, genuinely, though wrongly, believed to be real). So perhaps I should have extended the treatment to them as well, as some have assumed I did. But the use of natural language as a guide perhaps reveals an essential difference.

I have some sort of memory of Michael Dummett having stated in a lecture that names often regarded as simply empty are in fact names of fictional characters. I cannot at the moment verify this, nor the relation of his views to those in my lectures. But if this memory is correct, then Dummett deserves credit as an inspiration for these lectures. In fact, in the discussion session of my paper "Vacuous Names and Fictional Entities" (a precursor of these lectures, now published in *Philosophical Troubles*), Dummett said: "What you talked about this morning mostly related to overt fiction intended as such and, indeed, recognized as such. And I go along with much of what you said about that." (The discussion took place in March of 1973 and was subsequently published as the "Second General Discussion Session" in *Synthese*).[1] And in the same year, in his book on Frege, he writes:

> We should not, as Frege often does, cite as examples of names having sense but no reference personal names used in fiction, for these have in fact only a partial sense, since there is no saying what would warrant identifying actual people as their bearers; while the use of a name in literary criticism to refer to a fictional character differs again from its use *in* fiction, for here, while the sense is quite specific, the reference does not fail.
>
> (Dummett 1973: 160)

All this is quite consistent with my position, although the reader would find this brief statement difficult to follow.[2] However, if my memory of his influence on my views is correct, I must have heard him make similar claims on some previous occasion.[3]

Although the present lectures were never formally published until now, the transcript has been available at the Oxford University library for many years,[4] and it has had, since then, a modest life of its

---

1. Dummett et al. (1974: 511). My thanks to Romina Padró for this reference.
2. My thanks to Gary Ostertag for this reference. Dummett gives, as examples of genuinely empty names, 'Vulcan' (attributed to Geach); a fictitious Stanford student (concocted by real students) whom the administration for an entire semester was convinced actually existed; and another, hypothetical example.
3. I also want to mention that, independently of these lectures, Peter van Inwagen has published two papers advocating a very similar view. (See van Inwagen 1977 and 1983.) I haven't made any detailed comparison.
4. Unfortunately, the tapes of the lectures have not been preserved and, as far as I know, no record of the question periods exists.

own, passed on among members of the profession, sometimes even being discussed and criticized in print. One such case is Nathan Salmon's work. In various writings,[5] he has argued that I ought to have made greater and more effective use of the ontology of fictional characters I propose. Instead of saying that Conan Doyle only *pretends* to name any one entity, why not say that he *does* name one entity—the fictional character? The pretense is to name an actual person. (I think some other people may have taken me this way to begin with.) Salmon also wishes to extend the view to other such cases of fictional or mythological entities. I do not choose to evaluate this view here. I probably have not decided what I think. (Salmon himself recounts the skeptical reactions he has sometimes received.) At the moment I am inclined to believe that there may be problems with some aspects of his account.[6]

Many people have helped bring these lectures to print. They were originally transcribed by Henry Hardy, and I want to thank him for his work and for his insistence that they appear. Many colleagues, students, and members of the audiences where these lectures were presented have made remarks and contributions, and I have tried, to the best of my recollection, to acknowledge them in the relevant places. I hope I will be forgiven if I have forgotten to mention someone or include some contributions.

As it was the case with *Philosophical Troubles*, the Saul Kripke Center (SKC) at The Graduate Center of The City University of New York proved crucial for the publication of the present lectures. In particular, I would like to thank Gary Ostertag for editing the material and for helpful suggestions, and especially Romina Padró

---

5. See Salmon (1987), (1998), and (2002). Similar views are also defended by Amie Thomasson (see Thomasson 1996 and 1999).

6. It should be added that even Salmon thinks that there are cases of genuine empty names. And see the case of 'Sam Jones' in my own text.

for putting together a first draft, and for her comments, advice, and encouragement during the rewriting process. It was their enthusiasm for the material that finally persuaded me that it ought to appear. Working with them and the other members of the SKC, especially Jeff Buechner and Monique Whitaker, has been, as always, a pleasure.

I am grateful to the administration of the Graduate Center for their interest in my work. In particular, I would like to thank Provost Chase Robinson and my chair, Iakovos Vasiliou, for giving me time off to finish the book.

The proposal to publish the lectures was very well received by my editor at Oxford University Press, Peter Ohlin, and two anonymous referees. I am grateful to Peter, as well as the referees—you know who you are, and I think I know it, too. Peter's staff at OUP has been, once again, very helpful.

Finally, I would like to thank my father who, *pace* his many years, still manages to be interested in my progress.

REFERENCE AND EXISTENCE

October 30, 1973

I hope the title of these lectures gives some indication of their content. A while ago, in another place, I gave some lectures called "Naming and Necessity."[1] I wish here to continue with some of the topics I discussed there, in order to tie up some loose ends. I don't know to what extent I can presuppose the contents of those lectures;[2] perhaps I will get a clearer picture of that when the audience has jelled, so to speak. But I wish especially to discuss two areas which I didn't have the time and space to cover in *N&N*, and to raise a couple of topics related to them. One of them, which is perhaps the more important of the two, is the whole topic of how naming relates to existence, in particular the problem of vacuous names and reference to what does not exist, of fictional entities, of existential statements, and the like.[3] The other area which I intend to cover (I say "intend" advisedly because the work on the first topic may expand or contract) is that of speaker's reference and

---

1. Henceforth, *N&N*. The lectures were given at Princeton University in 1970 and were first published in 1972 as part of a larger collection edited by Donald Davidson and Gilbert Harman. They subsequently appeared in book form in 1980. See Kripke (1972/1980).
2. Remember that when the present lectures were given, in 1973, *N&N* was only recently published. I suppose that now the reader has a considerable advantage over the audience then, though some must have been familiar with the earlier work, or I wouldn't have been invited to give the John Locke Lectures!
3. These topics are discussed more briefly in "Vacuous Names and Fictional Entities" (Kripke 2011b), a precursor to these lectures given earlier in 1973 at a conference at the University of Connecticut.

semantic reference.[4] By "speaker's reference" I mean reference as used in such a phrase as 'Jones was referring to Smith when he said "that fat old hypocrite"'—this is reference by a speaker. The other related notion of semantic reference would be used in such a statement as: 'the phrase "the author of *Waverley*" refers in English to Sir Walter Scott.' This pair of topics is suggested by Donnellan (1966). Now let me start out with the first of these major topics.

No problem has seemed to represent a more perplexing philosophical conundrum than that of the use of names which have no reference—or, not to beg the question against Meinong (though I will beg it perhaps practically from here on out); names which appear to have no reference. We can also use names for imaginary entities. The fact that we can do so has been taken to be an almost conclusive argument in favor of one philosophical view as opposed to another. Mill, as I suppose most of us know, held that proper names had denotation but not connotation: when you use a name its semantic function consists simply in referring to an object, and nothing else. It does not refer to the object by giving it properties which pick the object out as a descriptive phrase does. If you call a man 'the man who corrupted Hadleyburg,' you have referred to him by virtue of describing him as the (unique) man who corrupted Hadleyburg.[5] But if you simply call him 'Sam,' you have simply called him that and have attributed no properties to him. The contrary view was taken both by Frege and by Russell as applied to what are ordinarily called 'proper names' in English. According to Frege

---

4. The material on this distinction was subsequently published in Kripke (1977). The matter is also discussed briefly in *N&N* (1972/1980: 25, note 3 and the accompanying text).

5. I had in mind the story by Mark Twain, actually titled "The Man that Corrupted Hadleyburg." When I gave these lectures (and also in *N&N*; see Kripke 1972/1980: 28), I replaced 'that' by 'who,' not remembering the original title. I still think that 'who' is what accords with natural English idiom, and do not know why Mark Twain used 'that' in the title. So I have decided to leave 'who' in the text.

and Russell, a proper name doesn't differ from a definite description in this respect. It too assigns certain properties that uniquely characterize the object, and the object is picked out as *the* object which has these properties. It isn't just simply a term without any descriptive content, or connotation, as Mill thought.

One of the things that seemed to be crucial in favor of the view of Frege and Russell here, as opposed to that of Mill, was the problem of existence. For we can surely, for example, raise the question whether Moses really existed, and even, if you like (though we would probably be wrong in this case in doing so), come up with a negative answer. But if someone concludes that Moses never existed, she surely is not using this name with the semantic function simply of referring to an object, and then denying of that object that it has the property of existence.[6] On the contrary, she is simply saying that there is no such object. If Mill were right, and the whole function of naming were simply reference, it seems hard to see how she could make such a statement or raise such a question. Once she used the name, she would be presupposing that there was an object to be referred to; she couldn't in addition ask about 'it' whether it existed or not. Much less could she conclude that 'it' doesn't really exist, that there is no such thing.

This in particular has been held to be conclusive against any kind of Millian paradigm. Also, of course, we can use proper names—as when we raise the question of whether Moses existed—without knowing whether they have reference or not. Moreover, we can make definite statements such as: 'If Moses really existed, he was not born in the Renaissance, since a book about him was written

6. 'Moses (Napoleon, etc.) no longer exists' strikes me as true, and expressing the fact that the individual referred to is dead, no longer with us, even though he once was. To my ear, the simple 'Moses (Napoleon, etc.) does not exist' is not the best way to express the matter. In my own discussions, I always imagine the question as being whether the entity *ever* existed.

before the Renaissance—somewhat before.' And we can also, of course, use names without thinking that they have reference at all. This is what goes on in fictional discourse when we talk about Sherlock Holmes, refer to Sherlock Holmes, and the like.

Frege and Russell gave a fairly uniform and common solution to this problem, which I suppose you all know. They in good part arrived at it independently. They had two doctrines (or maybe four?). First, they held that existence is not a first-level but a second-level concept (this is to use Frege's terminology as opposed to Russell's). By this they meant that although we meaningfully use the word 'exists' to say of a property or predicate that it is or is not instantiated, as when we say that there are tigers, and that there are no round squares—that tigers exist, but round squares do not[7]—the word 'exists' here expresses, so to speak, a property of properties, whether they are instantiated or not: it holds of a property if it is instantiated. This is what Frege calls a "second-level" concept.[8] To deny that it is a first-level concept is to deny that there is a meaningful existence predicate that can apply to objects or particulars. One cannot, according to Frege and Russell, say *of an object* that it exists or not because, so they argued, everything exists: how can one then divide up the objects in the world into those which exist and those which don't?

Russell talks about this in the lectures "The Philosophy of Logical Atomism." In the discussion following the fifth lecture, someone asks the following:

---

7. We could call these "plural existence statements": they assert or deny, as the case may be, that a property or predicate is instantiated.

8. For Frege this statement wasn't really strictly accurate, since he held that concepts were 'unsaturated' and were extensional; this doesn't agree with contemporary usage of the term 'properties.' These details don't matter for present purposes; the statement above gets the relevant ideas across.

Q: Is there any word you would substitute for 'existence' which would give existence to individuals? Are you applying the word 'existence' to two ideas, or do you deny that there are two ideas?

(Russell 1988a: 211)

That is, are there two ideas, one, *existence* as applied to concepts where the concept is instantiated, and the other, *existence* as applied to individuals in statements that would say of an individual that it exists? Russell answers:

Mr. Russell: No, there is not an idea that will apply to individuals. As regards the actual things there are in the world, there is nothing at all that you can say about them that in any way corresponds to this notion of existence. It is a sheer mistake to say that there is anything analogous to existence that you can say about them. [. . .] There is no sort of point in a predicate which could not conceivably be false. I mean, it is perfectly clear that, if there were such a thing as this existence of individuals that we talk of, it would be absolutely impossible for it not to apply, and that is the characteristic of a mistake.

(1988a: 211)[9]

Second, however, it seems that in ordinary language we clearly do talk as if we applied existence to individuals. For example,

---

9. As I said, Frege, too, held that existence is not a predicate of individuals. He thought that the fundamental error in the ontological argument was that it treated existence as a first level concept. (See Frege 1997b: 146.)

   Another relevant quotation is this: "I do not want to say it is false to say about an object what is said here about a concept; I want to say it is impossible, senseless, to do so. The sentence 'There is Julius Caesar' is neither true nor false but senseless; the sentence 'There is a man whose name is Julius Caesar' has a sense, but here again we have a concept, as the indefinite article shows" (Frege 1997d: 189). (In the second sentence, according to Frege's usual practice, one ought to put 'Julius Caesar' in quotation marks, but I am quoting from the translation given.)

someone can raise the question whether Napoleon really existed. The nineteenth-century logician Richard Whately raised this question in his book *Historic Doubts Relative to Napoleon Buonaparte* (Whately 1832), and concluded that Napoleon undoubtedly didn't exist because, as Hume argued, you shouldn't accept a story if it is too fantastic—it is more reasonable to suppose that people are lying (and, in this case, the story is quite fantastic).[10] The idea which applies here has of course been applied to the Gospels, too. (This was Hume's intent, though he more explicitly discusses the Pentateuch.) Anyway, one can raise the question whether Napoleon really ever existed, and in this case give an affirmative answer, though maybe some historian would come up with a negative one sometimes. (Whately did, or at least pretended to do so, and it is at any rate logically conceivable that he was right.) But we are at least *raising* the question of existence of an individual.

Frege and Russell, again as I suppose most of you know, answered this question by their analysis of proper names. To each proper name, they held, there corresponds a criterion or property picking out which individual is supposed to be named by the name. So, in the case of Napoleon, such a criterion might be 'being the leader of the forces that were defeated at Waterloo,' or various other things, fantastic things that we have heard about Napoleon. (Actually that one was not so fantastic.) The name will mean: '*the* thing which satisfies the criterion in question.' One can affirm the existence of Napoleon, meaning by it that the concept 'being defeated at the Battle of Waterloo' is uniquely instantiated—that is, that the concept 'being *the* one and only person who was the leader of the defeated forces' is instantiated.

---

10. This piece was of course actually a polemical spoof against Hume's essay "Of Miracles" (Hume 1975). The point was that on Hume's principles, one would just as well conclude that Napoleon was a fictitious or non-existent figure. It is clear from the piece itself that Napoleon was still alive when it was written.

So, according to Frege and Russell, the solution is as follows: with each proper name one associates some predicate that is supposed to be uniquely instantiated. If in fact there is a thing A which uniquely instantiates the property in question, then one says that Napoleon exists, or, in the general case, that A exists; if not, one says that A does not exist. But one is never really affirming *of an object* that it exists or not; one is instead affirming or denying of a *predicate* that it is uniquely instantiated. And this seems to correspond, of course, with the facts. What would a historian be doing if he asked whether Napoleon really existed? He wouldn't first find Napoleon and then look at him very carefully to see whether or not he really existed. Rather, he would see whether there was any one person who answers to the properties in the stories we have heard about Napoleon, or, at any rate, most, or "enough," of them.

This general doctrine presumably applies to the particular case where what we have before us may be a literary or mythological work, or a historical report, but we don't know which. Say we have the story about Moses: what do we mean when we ask whether Moses really existed? We are asking whether there is any person who has the properties—or at least enough of them—given in the story. In a famous passage in *Philosophical Investigations*, Wittgenstein, talking about this very case, says that we mean various things when we say that Moses did not exist, namely that the Israelites did not have a *single* leader when they withdrew from Egypt, or that their leader was not called 'Moses,' or that there could not have been anyone who accomplished all that the Bible relates of Moses, and so on. "I shall perhaps say," Wittgenstein says, "by 'Moses' I understand the man who did what the Bible relates of Moses, or at any rate, a good deal of it" (1953: §79). Here Wittgenstein is following Frege and Russell. He *does* want to modify them in one respect, in allowing that there is a cluster of properties picking the person out, rather than just a single one, and that this cluster will have rough edges: that is, there will be indeterminate cases in which it is impossible to say whether we would conclude that Moses existed or not. But the divergence here is unimportant for my purposes. Many moderns (by 'moderns' I mean people who are alive today)[11] have followed Wittgenstein in thinking that this would be one respect in which Frege and Russell need modification.

Thus, according to the orthodox doctrine, when we have, let's say, a literary work before us, or a history that may be historical reports or may be fiction, we know nothing else about a person apparently named in such a story other than what occurs in this story. Then—and this is the paradigm which has been generally accepted—to affirm the existence of, say, Sherlock Holmes, is to say that there is a unique person satisfying the properties attributed to Holmes in the story. To deny Holmes's existence is to say that there isn't any such person, or any such unique person, anyway (maybe there are ten of them, and we couldn't say which one was Holmes). This then is the orthodox doctrine.[12]

One should pay tribute to the power of the Frege-Russell analysis here. Actually, in the case of existence the analysis is even more powerful in Russell's version, I would say, than in Frege's.

---

11. That is, in 1973. I could have mentioned Searle (1958), as I did in *N&N*.

12. Although I take the Frege-Russell doctrine to analyze names in fiction according to the same paradigm that Frege used for 'Aristotle,' the name of a historical figure—that is as the unique person (or other object) fulfilling the story—I now find it hard to find an explicit statement in Frege about the senses of names in fiction. For example, he says "Although the tale of William Tell is a legend and not history and the name 'William Tell' is a mock proper name, we cannot deny it a sense" (Frege 1997c: 230). But he says little as to what this sense is. Similarly, talking about *The Odyssey*, he says that "the name 'Nausicaa,' which probably does not stand for [*bedeutet*] or name anything, . . . behaves as if it names a girl, and it is thus assured of a sense. And for fiction the sense is enough" (Frege 1997a: 178). But once again he does not specify what this sense is. The view that I have called the Frege-Russell doctrine on fiction does appear to me definitely to be held by Alonzo Church, a more recent Fregean.

That is, it is more unified, because Russell *in general* analyses out descriptions and names in favor of predicates, and the analysis comes out in precisely the same way in the case of the existence statements as in any other case. In the Frege version, the existence statements would have to be treated a bit specially, as when one analyses the question of whether Moses really existed or not.

The power of the Frege-Russell doctrine, which explains why it has so uniformly held the field in philosophy since then—perhaps until recently—has been the way it gives clear and uniform solutions to a variety of problems, of which this was one. It similarly analyses puzzles about identity statements, about reference in intensional contexts, and about just how names and singular terms can get a reference at all. It analyses them in a singularly uniform way which seems to treat every different case successfully.[13] Any theory which tries to give an alternative account has got to show what is wrong with this beautiful picture, and put forward an alternative and equally powerful picture in its place. This is what I am trying to make a start at doing in *N&N*.

In those lectures I presented a view that differs from that of Frege and Russell, and is closer, at any rate, to that of Mill in various respects. To say everything in the famous Talmudic phrase—I don't know if any of you have ever heard of it—"standing on one foot," the views discussed in *N&N* differ from that of Frege and Russell, particularly in the following ways.

13. However, this way of putting things glosses over a great deal, since it is well-known that Frege and Russell had very different views of definite descriptions. Frege applied the sense-reference distinction to definite descriptions, and held that the reference changes in intensional contexts, whereas Russell (as we would see him today) analyzes definite descriptions as complex quantifiers (actually defined in terms of the universal quantifier and truth-functions and identity), and gives a different solution to the problem of intensional contexts. (For some of my own discussion of these topics see Kripke 2005 and 2008.) In *N&N*, I constantly refer to the Frege-Russell doctrine, mostly having in mind what they would hold in common about (ordinary) proper names of historical figures, or names of fictional characters, etc. In the present lectures, I have especially in mind how both would deny that existence is a predicate of particulars.

First, I held that proper names, as opposed to most definite descriptions, are *rigid*. According to Frege and Russell, a proper name means a definite description. For example, the name 'Moses' means, let's say, 'the man who led the Israelites out of Egypt.' If that is what the name 'Moses' means, and if we wished to talk about a situation in which some other man had led the Israelites out of Egypt, then in using the name 'Moses' in counterfactual situations, we would be using it to refer to the man who *in those situations* would have led the Israelites out of Egypt, and this would not be Moses himself. Thus, according to Frege and Russell, if their analysis were correct, such a name as 'Moses' would be *non-rigid*. It would refer to different people in different situations. On the contrary, I argued, when we use the name 'Moses' it always means or refers to *the* man, the particular man, who—I suppose they are right about the rest— *in fact* led the Israelites out of Egypt. Actually I reject their view on this question too, but let us accept it for a moment. So 'Moses' is to mean '*the* man who in fact led the Israelites out of Egypt.' We use the name 'Moses' rigidly to refer to a certain man, and we use it to refer to that man even when talking about counterfactual situations in which the man didn't lead the Israelites out of Egypt.

This is one respect in which I think that Frege and Russell were wrong, and Mill would have been right: Frege and Russell would have affirmed that such a statement as 'Moses led the Israelites out of Egypt'—or, in Wittgenstein's modification, 'Moses, if he existed, did many of the things the Bible relates of him'—is analytic and therefore presumably a necessary truth, whereas it seems to me to be plainly a contingent truth. Some other man than Moses might have done all these things, and Moses might have done none of them. In that case it would have been false; it would not have been the case. So, far from being analytic, it is not true in all possible worlds.

Second, I held that even in determining reference in the actual world—and this is a different issue—we do not generally use properties that we believe to be satisfied by the objects to pick them out. Rather, some picture like this is to be held: someone initially 'baptizes' the object, picking out the object perhaps by pointing to it, or perhaps by its properties, or perhaps by some other device. Then—I follow Mill here—speakers wish only to preserve the reference of the name, and as the name is passed from link to link, if one person wishes to use it in the same way as she heard it, she uses it with the same reference as the speaker from whom she heard it. The name gets spread throughout the community, and down through history, with only the reference preserved. All sorts of myths may arise about the object which are not really true of it. It may even become the case that the great bulk, or perhaps all of what is believed uniquely to identify the object, in fact fails to apply to it. I tried to substantiate this by a battery of counterexamples to the usual view. I don't think that I will go into them at this point, but I might review them later.

One question which I didn't treat was the very question of existence, and I wish to fill this lacuna here—the questions are in fact very elaborate. But before I do so let me say a little bit more about what Russell in particular held about empty names and existence. Russell, unlike Frege (here I take back everything I said about him before!), agreed with Mill that proper names have denotation but not connotation. Where I spoke of the Frege-Russell view as opposed to that of Mill, I perhaps should have spoken of the *Mill-Russell* view as opposed to that of Frege. I was therefore slightly inaccurate. Why did I speak in that way? Because when you come up with anything that anyone would ordinarily call a name, Russell (even this is somewhat inaccurate) would agree with Frege about it as against Mill. Russell would hold that such a name does have a sense given by a descriptive phrase. (He really held that there is no such thing as Fregean sense, but let's leave that out: the divergence isn't important here. See note 13.) But then, since he officially agrees with Mill, he holds that the things that we ordinarily call 'names' aren't really names, and that we have to leave it to analysis to discover what the genuine names really are.

One of the criteria that are demanded by this argument to apply to names—genuine names of genuine objects—is that they have to name objects such that we can't even meaningfully raise the question about whether they exist. In particular, it cannot be subject even to Cartesian doubt whether such objects exist. Now Russell thought you could have an inventory of which objects could be named, which are, in his own terminology, objects of acquaintance. The most plausible candidates for this were one's own immediate sense-data; for one's immediate sense-data are things which are not subject to Cartesian doubt—by definition.[14] If I have a sense-datum of a yellow

---

14. Some years ago, long after the present lecture was delivered, Gideon Makin emphasized to me that for Russell sense-data were something physical. See the first sections of "The Relation of Sense-data to Physics" (Russell 1917b). Since this paper was written reasonably close to the lectures I am quoting, it is probable that Russell has not changed his mind. Exactly what types of physical entities he has in mind in this paper is rather obscure to me, but it does not seem to affect the main discussion in the present lecture. They are indubitable objects of acquaintance and are relatively fleeting.

I should add that in saying that Russellian sense-data are not open to *Cartesian* doubt I was influenced by Anscombe's formulation that "the bearers of the only genuine proper names are existents not open to Cartesian doubt (Russell's objects of immediate acquaintance—sense-data, etc.)" (Anscombe 1959: 43). This formulation is of course strictly meaningless according to Russell, since it uses existence as a predicate of the sense-data. Nevertheless, I think it captures what Russell had in mind in his doctrine of acquaintance with sense-data. Russell writes:

> Some of our beliefs turn out to be erroneous, and therefore it becomes necessary to consider how, if at all, we can distinguish knowledge from error. This problem does not arise with regard to knowledge by acquaintance, for, whatever may be the object of acquaintance, even in dreams and hallucinations, there is no error involved so long as we do not go beyond the immediate object: error can only arise when we regard the immediate object, i.e. the sense-datum, as the mark of some physical object. (Russell 1912: 110)

speck in front of me, I can be in no doubt, or no *Cartesian* doubt, as to whether it really exists. In that case there is no point in raising the question whether it exists, and the question whether *this*—this yellow speck in front of me—exists, can simply be dismissed as meaningless, if one wants, because there is no issue to be raised.

Russell also thought at various times that there were other objects of acquaintance, genuinely nameable. One example, when he believed in such an entity, might be the Cartesian self.[15]

It would seem that once a sense-datum or visual impression has disappeared, it won't have the status of a nameable object, because one may, as Russell was well-known for arguing, mistrust one's memory about whether such a thing really existed after all. Once again in the lectures on logical atomism Russell emphasizes his belief. In the question period, he is asked:

Question: If the proper name of a thing, a "this," varies from instant to instant, how is it possible to make any argument?

(1988a: 180)

The point is that if Russell is right, the objects which can be genuinely named are very fleeting. Once you move your head, things are not the same, and according to this theory one has altogether a new set of objects to be named 'Sam,' 'Harry,' and so on. So how can you

---

15. In the paper "Knowledge by Acquaintance and Knowledge by Description," published originally in 1910, Russell speaks of genuine proper names, that is, "words which do not assign a property to an object, but merely and solely name it," and claims that "there are only two words which are strictly proper names of particulars, namely, 'I' and 'this'" (Russell 1917a: 162). However, in a footnote added in 1917, he says: "I should now exclude 'I' from proper names in a strict sense, and retain only 'this'" (see page 162, note 2). The category of genuine proper names, naming objects of acquaintance, now seems to be that of "The Philosophy of Logical Atomism." In general, his picture of genuine objects of acquaintance seems to have narrowed progressively since he introduced it in "On Denoting," though it was rather narrow there already.

make a deductive argument? For if the premise contains names, the conclusion will contain these very same names, and no longer be a part of the language when you are through. He replies:

> Mr. Russell: You can keep "this" going for about a minute or two. I made that dot [he had then put a dot on the blackboard] and talked about it for some little time. I mean it varies often. If you argue quickly, you can get some little way before it is finished. I think things last for a finite time, a matter of some seconds or minutes or whatever it may happen to be.
>
> Question: You do not think that air is acting on that and changing it?
>
> Mr. Russell: It does not matter about that if it does not alter its appearance enough for you to have a different sense-datum.
>
> (1988a: 180)

It is only the sense-datum that matters—however, you would better be careful to hold still. I could not do it. This picture may seem rather fantastic; nevertheless I have not found in subsequent philosophy an adequate reply to the arguments that moved Russell to such an answer.

Wittgenstein took the argument up in the *Tractatus*. He held that nameable objects (he called them simply "objects," whereas Russell called them "particulars") had to be part of the necessary furniture of the world, things that could not have failed to exist. Those things which have only contingent existence are not really objects—they are combinations of genuine objects. By this I mean not that the real objects are molecules, or something like that, but that when we say that this table might not have existed, of course we mean that the molecules comprising it might not have been formed in the combination that appears as this table. They might have had another arrangement. And that is what we mean whenever we talk about contingent existence.[16] But the genuine objects are part of the necessary furniture of the world—they are the same in all possible worlds. And this too seems to follow from the arguments. Because if the only function of naming is reference, and we can't even raise the question of existence, then we can't say that an object might not have existed; we can't speak of the contingency of the fact that it does—to do this would be to make singular existence statements meaningful—as Moore pointed out (see next lecture).

Wittgenstein is following Frege and Russell—and here, I think, especially Russell. It is interesting to note that the two require-ments that they place on the existence of these objects—one, indubitability, and the other, the Wittgensteinian requirement that they have necessary existence—are incompatible.[17] For it would seem, at least to me, that nothing more plainly has contingent exis-tence than one's own immediate sense-data, one's own immediate visual impressions. Right now I am having a bunch of them, but I might not have had these sense-data at all. How could I have avoided having them? Well, if the attendance at my lectures had been different, if I myself had not turned up, if I had come in and decided to talk with a blindfold. In any one of these cases I would have had not a single one of these sense-data. Or I could have been shot dead before the lectures began, or I might never have been

---

16. Obviously we shouldn't be misled by my example of the molecular theory, since this example depends on empirical considerations about physics. But the point is that any ques-tion of contingent existence must really be a question of whether objects do or do not relate to each other in various ways. The genuine simple objects are the same in all possible worlds.

17. In the beginning of the lectures "The Philosophy of Logical Atomism," Russell states that he is expounding ideas that he got from Wittgenstein. Some ideas may indeed reflect his influ-ence. The *Tractatus* had not been written yet (or at least, not seen by Russell), and Russell was in no contact with Wittgenstein, as he states. Probably the ideas in these lectures should really be attributed to Russell himself. As is well-known, when Russell did write an intro-duction to the *Tractatus*, Wittgenstein strongly disapproved of it and thought it superficial and a misunderstanding of his ideas.

born. So these entities certainly have contingent existence; if any entity has necessary existence, it isn't these.[18] Nor is the self a necessary existent either, for I might never have been born.

Something must have gone wrong here, for the requirements that are placed on the objects have led these two philosophers working together to conclusions which are incompatible and contradictory: it is essentially the same argument, first applied in the epistemological sphere, and second applied in, so to speak, the metaphysical sphere, which leads to the two conclusions.

It has been a bit of a question, in the exegesis of the *Tractatus*, whether Wittgenstein's objects are in fact Russellian objects, whether they are in fact one's own immediate perceptions, or at least include them. I don't want to go into an exegetical question, and perhaps couldn't conclusively argue this, but it would seem that if Wittgenstein had his wits about him on this matter, the objects couldn't be one's own immediate sense-data, because such objects would fail to satisfy the most elementary requirements of the theory. Therefore, unless he simply failed to notice this, he didn't believe that these were the objects. Of course, people can fail to notice things, so perhaps the argument isn't conclusive.

Anyway, people did seem to fail to notice that one and the same argument leads to two conclusions which are quite incompatible. I know of no object that I could mention, at least among the relevant particulars, which would satisfy the criterion both of necessary

18. I must admit that in the argument I give here I was certainly not aware of Russell's notion of 'sensibilia' as set out in Russell (1917b). According to that paper, though *sensibilia* become sense-data only in virtue of a person getting acquainted with them, they exist anyway, as what would have been seen, etc. from a certain perspective. Thus the fact that someone's sense-data would not exist if he were not looking a certain way is only analogous to the fact that no man can be a husband without getting married. I find this doctrine of the real existence of *sensibilia* rather confusing, but since they are supposed to be physical objects, I would take it that they do not have necessary existence. None of this is mentioned in Russell (1988a).

existence and of indubitable existence. (Well, perhaps the statement should be rather stronger: I know for certain of no object which is a particular and which satisfies just the single criterion of necessary existence.)[19] Since there are these incompatible conclusions something must be wrong with the analysis; but that is not to say what.

It is interesting to notice this case because very often the idea of epistemological certainty or a priority (really these two epistemological notions are not to be identified with each other) has been identified with that of necessity. I inveigh against this very strongly in N&N. In particular, I say that, even if it were indubitable that Moses really existed, that he must actually have done most of the things related of him in the Bible, that is not to say that the statement that, if Moses existed, he did these things, is a necessary truth, for in counterfactual situations it would have been false. Anyway, in this case the divergence is so great that one is led to sweepingly incompatible conclusions.

Now I want to say something else about and against Russell at this point. He introduces his very special category of logically proper names in order to solve a philosophical problem: since one cannot meaningfully ask of a particular whether it exists—for if one is referring to a particular, then of course it exists—Russell wishes to create a special category of particulars which can be named and which indubitably exist. This is supposed to eliminate the need to analyze negative existential statements for this special case. Negative existential statements arise in particular when we discuss fiction. We say that Sherlock Holmes, Dick Tracy (is he known in this country?), Jupiter, and Pegasus do not really exist. They occur in fiction. Russell doesn't want to have a realm of fictional existence, so he analyses these statements as: 'no unique thing satisfies the

19. Well, some have argued that the Deity is a particular that necessarily exists.

conditions laid down in the story.' In the case of genuine names for immediate sense-data this problem is not supposed to arise, and that is why he creates this category. Well, I think he failed to avoid the problem for this very case, even if one agrees with him that the existence of one's own immediate sense-data is not subject to Cartesian doubt, so that the question of existence cannot meaningfully be raised.

Ordinarily, when I tell a story I fill it with names of people, but in this case let us suppose that I am a Russellian who likes to use Russellian logically proper names. I am still writing a story, so I write it about immediate sense-data of mine; only in this case they can be imaginary. So I do not see a yellow speck over there, but I will write a story for myself, for my own use, in which I suppose that I do, and give it the proper name 'Matilda.' This, in the context of the story, would represent me as fulfilling a perfectly legitimate Russellian process of naming. Now, commenting to myself about this story, pointing out that it is only a story, I say 'Well, of course Matilda doesn't really exist.' Because it is only a story, I am not having a sense-datum of a yellow speck in front of me, though I then go on to tell the story about what is happening to me as a result of seeing this yellow speck. The story could contain even a name of an actual sense-datum,[20] say 'Aloysius,' and I would say that Aloysius really does exist. Just because something occurs in the story, it does not mean that the entity so named is fictional. There are fictional stories, for example, about Napoleon—a real person—and in commenting on those stories one says that Napoleon really existed, but his faithful dog Fido in the story did not—he is from the fictional part. So here too I could say: 'So, Aloysius really exists; Matilda does not.'

20. Here and throughout this discussion, I am writing as if the Russellian notion of sense-datum were clear and uncontroversial. But I do not commit myself to this.

This is a perfectly good comment to make, and it uses in the one case a genuine Russellian proper name, 'Aloysius,' and in the other case a putative such name, 'Matilda,' which is being asserted here to be only fictional. It does so for precisely the same reasons as would apply if one were naming people, and precisely the same questions of analysis or proper account should arise.

One should not say here that 'Matilda' and 'Aloysius' are not really names: 'Aloysius' was stipulated to be such a genuine name—it is being contrasted here with 'Matilda'—and 'Matilda' too is a putative genuine Russellian proper name, but in fact it names nothing. One should not say that either of these are really definite descriptions. For one thing this would give a false account of the facts as I just stated them. For another, what definite descriptions could they be? Well, 'Aloysius' isn't supposed to be a definite description; I introduced it as the reverse. Perhaps then one could argue that 'Matilda' turns out really to be a definite description? Well, what definite description is it?

One candidate might be, 'the yellow speck I see in front of me'—say that it is really used as short for that. But that can't be right—the story might not assert at all that there is only one yellow speck in front of me. I'd be luckier perhaps if that were so, but it might say that there was a bunch of them, and pick one of them out, calling it 'Matilda.' So the name could not refer to *the* unique yellow speck I see in front of me, nor could 'Matilda' be analyzed as being '*the* thing I call "Matilda,"' because I may elsewhere in other contexts genuinely use 'Matilda' as the name of an ordinary woman, though I do not so use it here. Nor could it be used as equivalent to 'the yellow speck I call "Matilda."' Perhaps at some earlier time I called some yellow speck 'Matilda,' or perhaps even at the present time there is some yellow speck (even now in front of me) which I call 'Matilda.' But in the story I am not using 'Matilda' to refer to that speck: I am simply, because of my fondness for it, naming my fictional object after the speck. The same thing would more plausibly work with people. Of course, one can try to get around this with 'the thing that I call "Matilda" in this story,' where this very sentence occurs in the story, but one had better not go to that—at least in a hurry. The problems with such self-reference are well-known, and presumably one should not leap into them here.

At any rate, even aside from such arguments, I think such an account obviously falsifies the facts. What is going on in a story such as this one is that one is romancing to oneself that one is giving a genuine Russellian proper name to an object. Russell thinks he has solved the problem because, if he is right, the objects he names have indubitable existence. That gets rid of the problem of a possible *mistake*, that is, of thinking that there is a Napoleon when there isn't really one, but it does not get rid of the possibility of empty names and, hence, of negative existentials. It does not get rid of the possibility of *fictional* discourse containing such putative names. Therefore it does not get rid of negative existential statements, for though the answer to the question 'Does Matilda exist?' will be trivial—it will be obvious to the man who tells the story—still it will be negative. Matilda does not really exist; Aloysius does. One can draw this contrast, and so Russell does not avoid the problem.[21]

This particular argument against Russell seems to me to show something important. For the problem of singular negative existentials—of being able to say that *A* does not exist (say, that Moses does not exist)—was supposed to be an argument which was conclusive against any Millian type of paradigm, any paradigm

---

21. This can supplement the argument against Russell used by Moore (1959b: 126), which points to the fact that one's own immediate sense-data have contingent existence. See Lecture II, note 7 and accompanying text, for discussion.

which made the existence of a referent essential to the semantic function of naming. 'What about fiction?' it is immediately said. There are names which just don't refer.[22]

Just the contrary seems to be the case. The existence of fiction is a powerful argument for absolutely nothing: it cannot settle the question as between the Russellian theory and the Millian theory, nor can it settle the question between Mill's theory and any other theory. Take a semantic theory which says that the essential semantic properties of names are such-and-such—for example, the Millian theory, where having a referent is an essential feature of a name, or Russell's, where this is true for genuine proper names, but, as I said before, not for what we ordinarily call 'proper names.'[23] Suppose some criterion or other is given: now, what do you say about a fictional case? Doesn't that represent a big problem which can adjudicate between one theory and another? Isn't it a problem for Mill's theory, where there cannot be names with no referent, as appears to be the case in fiction? Well, *no*, I think it does not, because when one writes a work of fiction, it is part of the pretense of that fiction that the criteria for naming, whatever they are, are satisfied. I use the name 'Harry' in a work of fiction; I generally presuppose as part of that work of fiction, just as I am pretending various other things, that the criteria of naming, whatever they are—Millian or Russellian or what have you—are satisfied. That is part of the pretense of this work of fiction. Far from it being the case that a theory of the

22. Although some might argue that there are senses in which they really do. I will deal with that later.

23. It is also worth noting that Mill would have had to supplement his account by some theory or criterion of how the reference of a name is determined, for the answer cannot simple be just that we point—indeed, it's pretty clear that it's not generally the case that reference is determined that way. In my own case, where I held a view which is at any rate closer to Mill than that of his successors, if not entirely that of Mill, the criterion is given by a historical chain in which the reference is transmitted from link to link. But the answer really doesn't need to be dealt with here. (It is one of the main points of *N&N*.)

reference of names ought to make special provision for the possibility of such works of fiction, it can forget about this case, and then simply remark that, in a work of fiction, it is part of the pretense of that work of fiction that these criteria are satisfied. Perhaps what makes it a work of fiction is that these criteria are not in fact satisfied (and usually other things in the story), but the pretense is just that: a pretense.

So I will call this 'The Pretense Principle,' to give it a name.[24] If this is so, it would apply to any theory of naming whatsoever. And in particular, as I just pointed out, it applies even to Russell's notion of logically proper names. What is one doing in the fictional case? One is pretending as part of the work of fiction that one has a Russellian logically proper name here, and Russell does not avoid this possibility either. So, far from this being a crucial test case for theories of naming, it should be a test case for nothing whatsoever.

One can very well say that, as in Mill, it is an essential part of the semantic function of naming that there be a referent. Then, in a work of fiction, one pretends that this essential function is fulfilled. I do therefore—*if* I go by this principle—have to draw the consequence that, for a follower of Mill, the propositions that occur in a work of fiction would only be pretended propositions, so to speak. For example, if someone says 'Matilda is bothering me' in a work of fiction, what proposition is being expressed here? On Russell's view the proposition would contain as its constituents the thing 'Matilda,' and then relational properties, and maybe some other things, which

---

24. I think that many philosophers have observed that fiction is a pretense, and that the names occurring in it are pretenses of being names. However, when I gave the present lectures, I was unaware that Frege appears to be the first author explicitly to note this (see Frege 1997c: 229–30). I disagree with Frege on one point. When a proper name of a historical figure appears in a work of fiction, such as that of Napoleon in Tolstoy's *War and Peace*, Frege seems to think it does not really stand for Napoleon, whereas I think it does. For a fuller discussion, with the passage from Frege, see Kripke (2011b: 58, note 11).

correspond to the phrase 'bothering me.' But since there is no such thing as Matilda, there is no such proposition. One is simply pretending that there is. The same would go for the more general—or general-Millian—case, where it is being pretended that a more mundane referent, say a person, really exists, and propositions are being stated about him. Since there is no such person, there are no such propositions. (I will elaborate on this later.)

In the case of pretense in fiction there are some obvious qualifications. First, of course it need not be asserted in the work of fiction that the name used in the work of fiction is the character's name in the ordinary sense. In *Lolita*, Nabokov says, in fact, that the names have been changed to protect the innocent. Second, given a work of fiction, it need not in theory follow a correct philosophical theory of reference. Of course the work of fiction may fictionally say that some incorrect theory is the case. But this case is a rare exception probably arising only in theory. Normally a work of fiction will say no such thing, and can be assumed to provide no specific theory of reference.

This Pretense Principle, I think, would apply even if the Frege-Russell analysis were correct, and this shows how wrong the analysis has gone, as given in the orthodox version. Suppose Frege and Russell were right and the essential function of naming (in its ordinary use) *is* to give a descriptive property of an object, and thereby pick it out. I don't think it *follows*, anyway, that their analysis as adapted to the case of fictional works is correct. For remember their analysis. It says that a name in fiction means '*the* thing satisfying the properties stated in the story, or at any rate most of them—*the unique thing*.'[25] However, remember that the story is a pretense,

---

25. For example, in "On Denoting," Russell says that if we want to analyze sentences about 'Apollo,' we look at a classical dictionary and see that the phrase means 'the sun god' (see Russell 1905: 491).

pretending that the conditions for ordinary naming are satisfied. Then, all that should be required is that in the story it is presupposed that there are some properties by which the narrator picks the thing out, but *not* that these properties are stated in the story, or even, if the properties are stated, that they are given correctly. One can see clearly now what an incorrect account of the facts about fiction the Frege-Russell theory gives, even supposing it is correct in a non-fictional case.

First, it says that the proper name means '*the* thing satisfying the properties in the story.' To affirm existence is to affirm that there is a *unique* thing satisfying the properties in the story. This is radically false. Why the uniqueness? Why should the story say anything that even putatively identifies an object uniquely? It talks about, very fleetingly, a certain tall man, Sam Smith, who accosted the hero on the corner of some street. Now does that mean that only one tall man ever accosted the hero of the story on some street? Or it may say just that Sam Smith is a tall man and that the hero knew him: it says 'If I were a tall man like Sam Smith, I would be such-and-such.' Does that really imply that Sam Smith is the unique tall man, or even the unique tall man about whom the hero ever so mused? It need not even mean that there is a unique tall man *called 'Sam Smith'* about whom the hero so mused. Perhaps there are several. Still, he was represented as musing about a particular tall man, Sam Smith, on this particular occasion. The story need not even putatively assert uniqueness.

Second, it is held that if there is an object which uniquely satisfies the properties attributed to the object in a story, then it is not a story: the thing really exists, and the account is not fictional at all. But the common practice of authors is just the very reverse. They print at the beginning of their story: 'The names used in this story are fictional, and any resemblance to characters living or dead is

purely coincidental.' Suppose a person, believing himself to be pos-
sessed of a valid suit for invasion of privacy, sues the author of such
a story, and proves in court that he uniquely satisfies the properties
mentioned in that story. Then will the judge necessarily rule on
behalf of the plaintiff? I think not. Suppose the author can show that
he never heard of this man; that he definitely wasn't writing about
him; that it was indeed a coincidence, just as he said. Then a reasonable judge would rule against the plaintiff, against Frege, against
Russell, and against Wittgenstein, and hold that the author had a
valid defense, though this person uniquely fits the story.[26]

Finally, the other way around, Frege and Russell would claim
that if no person fits the story at all, then one can conclude that, say,
Sherlock Holmes does not exist. This is radically false. It fails to distinguish between a work of fiction about a historical person, and a
work of fiction about a fictional character. Take the Napoleon case
that I mentioned before. Suppose, in the year 3000, only one of
these fictional stories about Napoleon survives. Can one then conclude that Napoleon never existed, or at least that, as used in this
story, the name 'Napoleon' refers to no one? No, one cannot. This
story is still a story about a real man, although the only thing to
survive in this case is fictional. So I emphasized in N&N that,
though the case of Moses is not a counterexample, the case of Jonah
in the Bible may be. Some biblical scholars argue, and one can quote
them, that though the story about Jonah is entirely fictional, the

---

26. When I gave these talks, A. J. Ayer informed me (although he said it didn't affect the philosophical point I was making) that I was not correct in English law (which is very favorable
to plaintiffs in libel cases). I mentioned this in the discussion afterwards, and someone
remarked that I would be right in American law. Naturally, the greater the "coincidence"
involved (and the larger the corpus), as in the totality of the Sherlock Holmes stories, the
more unlikely it is that there should be some unique person who, by some coincidence,
matches these stories but has no connection with Conan Doyle. But, however unlikely it
may be, it is not impossible.

man Jonah really existed. This was one of the legendary accounts (unfortunately the real historical ones have not survived) about a genuinely existing Hebrew prophet.[27]

Since I am over time, I will stop here. I should mention that it is in the analysis of this very case that I think the Frege-Russell theory goes even more wrong—in the counterfactual situation. I will deal with that next time, not today as expected.

I have argued (a) that the Frege-Russell theory is not demanded by the existence of fictional works—in fact no particular theory is demanded—and (b) that, as it is stated, it solves the problems that it raises about these works incorrectly. I think that it even incorrectly applies itself to these works: one shouldn't say that one uses the predicates in the story; one should just say that it is part of the pretense of the story that there are such properties that pick the objects out, known to the narrator. Of course, to say these things is not to give a positive and correct account, since we haven't dealt with the problems about the existential statements and so on. And that, of course, will be the next important task.

27. See N&N (Kripke 1972/1980: 67, note 28). But maybe this wasn't the "scholarly consensus" I thought it was. I have since seen writers others than the one I quote state the contrary. It doesn't matter, since as I said, the view could be true, whether or not there was evidence for it.

Also, even at the time I gave the present lectures, though maybe I didn't know it then, I could have used Moses instead as an example. The famous biblical scholar Martin Noth thought that Moses was a historical figure, but (contrary to the impression one would get from Wittgenstein's discussion) that he had little to do with the exodus from Egypt, or most of the best-known things related about him in the Pentateuchal account. (The true core about him is "guidance into the arable land.")

Perhaps I should add that since then, I have read authors even more unfavorable to the historicity of the exodus. But these are questions not to be discussed here.

November 6, 1973

Last time I argued that the types of names which occur in fictional discourse are, so to speak, "pretended names," part of the pretense of the fiction. The propositions in which they occur are pretended propositions rather than real propositions; or rather, as we might put it, the sentences pretend to express a proposition rather than really doing so.

I also argued that, even if one reserved the term "proper name" for those which Russell would recognize as *logically* proper names (genuine as opposed to ordinary names), the same phenomenon would arise: in such a case there would also be a category of pretended names which occur in fiction, where I fancy or pretend that I name a Russellian sense-datum, or visual impression, or what have you. It is true that in the Russellian case the speaker of the language could regard these names as a separate semantical category, open to her own inspection, as long as the language is confined to herself. Then the speaker of the language can always tell whether she has genuinely named an object with which she is acquainted, or is simply pretending to do so. Nevertheless, there is this semantical category of pretended names. It would not be reducible to the category of definite descriptions according to any simple paradigm as the one Russell suggests, 'the thing satisfying most of the properties in the story.' One would be able to make statements such as 'Matilda does not exist, but Aloysius does,' using a pretended name 'Matilda' and a genuine logically proper name 'Aloysius' to make the contrast.

The problem of their analysis would be quite similar to that in the ordinary case where one admits that people, planets, ships, shoes, and sealing wax can be named. So why not try the same thing in the general case as one would in the Russellian special case?

One reason perhaps has been that people have assumed that what semantical category a term belongs to should be open to introspection by any user of the sentence. If one regards pretended names or fictive names as a semantical category separate from ordinary names, then the present account depends on denying this assumption. For in the case of ordinary fiction which is communicated to others, though it will be true perhaps that the author knows whether she is using a pretended name or really denoting an object—whether she is spinning fiction or telling the truth—her hearers may be under the wrong impression, or may be uncertain what is going on. And even the author herself may at an appropriate later time forget what she was doing. If so, then the hearer, or the author at a later date, will be under the mistaken impression that something is a name when in fact it is not: it is merely a pretended name.

So we also have to allow a category of mistakes that such and such is a name, and a category of mistakes that such and such a sentence genuinely expresses a proposition. This can happen not only when one is reading a work which one thinks not to be fiction when it is, or when one is unsure whether it is fiction or not: it can also happen in other ways as well. An example would be the naming by some astronomers of a hypothetical planet 'Vulcan' which was thought to cause certain perturbations in Mercury. It was later discovered that no such planet did cause these perturbations, and this paved the way for the general theory of relativity. Here the astronomers were, on my view, under a mistaken impression that they had named a planet when they introduced the name; and when they uttered sentences containing the name 'Vulcan' it was a *mistake* to suppose that they expressed propositions, rather than a case of pretense. And most of what I say about pretense, though not perhaps all (you can check it out for yourselves), will apply *mutatis mutandis* with the term 'mistake' in place of 'pretense.'

Last time I talked about what a bad analysis I thought the Frege-Russell view gave of our assertions that Moses does exist or that Sherlock Holmes does not. I said that their analysis of these statements, when they are asserted, as 'some unique person, who has most of the properties in such and such a story, exists' fails to take account of the correct logical properties involved. In fact, I argued that even if their theory of how reference was determined were correct they should not assume that to say that Sherlock Holmes existed would be to say that the properties in the story were satisfied. They should rather have the author *pretend* that there exist definite descriptions which determine the referent, though these descriptions need not be given in the story itself: the story may not specify anything which is even putatively uniquely identifying.

I want also to say how this view goes over for modal properties. How does the Frege-Russell analysis work here? I have argued in *N&N*, and would reiterate here, that in modal contexts the analysis comes off even worse. Frege and Russell (and Wittgenstein, who dealt with this particular example, as quoted in Lecture I) wish to hold that 'Moses exists' is to be analyzed as 'some one unique person led the Israelites out of Egypt' and so on—whatever else the Bible says. Let's just suppose for brevity that it is just leading the Israelites out of Egypt which is in question. Now how does this work out hypothetically, or rather, counterfactually? It seems to me that it works out especially badly in this case. For Moses could have existed even though no one led the Israelites out of Egypt. He himself might have existed and simply failed to do so, for whatever reason.[1] The converse fails also, of course. Some unique person might have led the Israelites out of Egypt, even if Moses had never been born. Someone else might have done so in his place. There might indeed be a view of history that one unique person is uniquely called forth by some kind of metaphysical principle to perform a destined task. One should not however attempt to prove this view simply by an analysis of proper names, and their connection with existence statements. But the analysis supposed here would do so.

I should mention in this connection a kind of reply that has naturally suggested itself to readers, and is in fact mentioned in *N&N*, but apparently not answered, or at any rate not answered to everyone's satisfaction, since I have gotten this reply in spite of its earlier mention. I sometimes use modal arguments to argue that, for example, 'Moses' cannot mean '*the* man who led the Israelites out of Egypt' because, after all, it might have been the case, as I just said, that Moses didn't lead the Israelites out of Egypt.

Now one reply to this has been in terms of the Russellian notion of the scope of a description. Suppose the term 'Moses' did abbreviate 'the man x who Led the Israelites Out of Egypt':

$$1.\ M = \imath x\, LIOE(x)$$

Now I can argue that 'Moses' doesn't mean this by saying that it is possible that Moses didn't lead the Israelites out of Egypt:

$$2.\ \Diamond \neg LIOE(M)$$

---

1. But see the views about the historical Moses mentioned in Lecture I, note 27. Here I can be taken to be assuming that the Pentateuchal account of Moses's role is substantially correct, at least enough of it to satisfy the conditions in the passage I cite from Wittgenstein.

Whereas it couldn't be possible that '*the* man who led the Israelites out of Egypt' didn't lead the Israelites out of Egypt:

$$3.\ \Box\neg\Diamond\neg\text{LIOE}(\imath x\ \text{LIOE}(x))$$

It can easily be pointed out that under Russell's theory of descriptions the statement represented by (2) has two interpretations, owing to Russell's notion of scope.[2] One interpretation says that it is possible that there is a man such that he was the only man who led the Israelites out of Egypt, and didn't do so:

$$4.\ \Diamond\,(\exists x)(\text{LIOE!}(x)\wedge\neg\text{LIOE}(x))$$

(The exclamation mark here is my own notation and means that x, and only x, led the Israelites out of Egypt.)[3] That is certainly a contradiction.

But there is another interpretation which would give the description the large scope: 'there is an x such that x in fact led the Israelites out of Egypt uniquely, and it is possible that *he* didn't':

$$5.\ (\exists x)(\text{LIOE!}(x)\wedge\Diamond\,\neg\text{LIOE}(x))$$

And that is not a contradiction. (4) says that it is possible that someone both led the Israelites out of Egypt and didn't: that is a contradiction. But it is not a contradiction to say that there is someone who led the Israelites uniquely out of Egypt and it is possible that he might not have.

In this case anyway, I don't in fact think this objection is correct if one goes through the details of my argument.[4] But I will leave it there.

---

2. For a more elaborate discussion of this notion see now Kripke (2005).

3. The exclamation point after a predicate has a different meaning in *Principia Mathematica*. ($\exists!x$) is often used to mean "there is a unique x," and this usage motivated the present notation, which is needed here.

4. In fact, as I have argued in the preface to *N&N*, the argument really applies to simple sentences, without modal operators. For more on this, see the preface to *N&N* (Kripke 1972/1980: 6–16).

Let me just speak of how it might apply to our special case, because here it seems to me to be especially weak as a defense of a descriptivist analysis of proper names. Suppose it was not 'Moses did not lead the Israelites out of Egypt' which was in question but 'Moses does not exist':

$$6. \; \neg E(M)$$

And now we want to speak of the possibility of this in modal contexts. For example, we might, superficially, write 'It might have been the case that Moses would not have existed,' as this:

$$7. \; \Diamond \neg E(M)$$

That is, he wouldn't have existed under certain circumstances. (I really should always be careful to use the subjunctive here, because that is what I mean. If you use the indicative you are generally speaking epistemically rather than counterfactually.) It is possible, then, that Moses wouldn't have existed under certain circumstances: Moses might not have existed.

Now, can we here use the Frege-Russell analysis of 'Moses' as the description 'the man who led the Israelites out of Egypt uniquely' to analyze (7)? If one runs it the way I want, one gets according to me the wrong analysis. The analysis that I was suggesting was that (7) would mean 'It is possible that there was not a unique person who led the Israelites out of Egypt':

$$8. \; \Diamond \neg E(\imath x \, LIOE(x)) \; [\text{or} \; \Diamond \neg (\exists x) \, (LIOE!(x))]$$

And this seems to me not to be an analysis of the original. But the alternative would be, if one tried to do it parallel to this case, to say 'There is a man who, in fact, uniquely led the Israelites out of Egypt, and it is possible that that person wouldn't have existed under certain circumstances':

$$9. \; (\exists x)(LIOE!(x) \wedge \Diamond \neg E(x))$$

That is, there is in fact someone who led the Israelites out of Egypt, and he might not have existed, say if his mother hadn't given birth to him, even if someone else did lead the Israelites out of Egypt.

The trouble with trying the same scope device here is that it violates the basic principle of Frege and Russell that existence is not a predicate of individuals, that it is a second-level rather than a first-level concept. Because of that, *this* analysis, at least, is ruled out. One can't say 'there is someone whom I identify as the unique person who led the Israelites out of Egypt and *he* might not have existed,' because '*he* might not have existed' here makes no sense by itself. There may be some way out of this, but it is not straightforward. And this is aside from any objections that might be raised to this argument in the general case.[5] One might think that the difficulty here is very special to the case of existence. I don't think it is particularly. I think it suggests that this is not the reply in the general case either, but rather that the term 'Moses,' as I argued, should be regarded not as abbreviating a description which can designate different objects in different possible worlds, but as rigidly designating a certain man of whom we then say that he might not have led the Israelites out of Egypt under certain circumstances, that he might not have existed under certain circumstances, and so on. So the Frege-Russell analysis is especially difficult to maintain in this particular case.[6]

5. Again, see the relevant pages in the preface to *N&N*.
6. Many have connected Russell's analysis with the Kantian doctrine that existence is not a predicate, and have even asserted that Russell gave a precise formulation of the doctrine (see, for example, Quine 1940: 151). I don't really wish to go into heavy Kantian exegesis, in which I am hardly competent—and maybe not even light Kantian exegesis. But I do want to say this. Kant also talks about the feeling that if existence were a predicate it would seem to apply analytically, whereas in fact assertions of existence are synthetic. But whatever his position is (and it is somewhat obscure) it doesn't seem to me, as far as I am able to read him, to be identifiable with that of Frege and Russell.

Kant says that existence is a *logical predicate* but not a *real predicate*, that when we deny existence of a subject we don't deny a predicate of it, but rather reject the subject together

So my view is that it is perfectly legitimate to attribute existence to individuals, whether Russellian sense-data or anything else. Moore already argued even in connection with Russellian sense-data—which, as we have seen in Lecture I, he regarded as the only proper particulars that can have logically proper names—that Russell was wrong in concluding that no meaning could be given to existence as a predicate of individuals, since "it would be impossible for it not to apply, and this is the characteristic of a mistake." Moore says:

> [I]n the case of every sense-datum which anyone ever perceives, the person in question could always say with truth of the sense-datum in question 'This might not have existed'; and I cannot see how this could be true, unless the proposition 'This does in fact exist' is also true, and therefore the words 'This exists' significant.
>
> (1959b: 126)

Here I am in agreement with Moore's argument, as opposed to Russell and Frege.[7] It must be perfectly legitimate to attribute existence to individuals, because one can intelligibly say that they might not have existed. I myself do not restrict the point to Russellian sense-data, though Moore did so because he wished to follow Russell in thinking of these as

---

with *all* its predicates. But he nowhere, as far as I know from a very cursory study, says that existence doesn't apply to things at all, that it is only a second-level property which really applies to concepts. He just says that when we apply existence to or deny it of an individual we are not doing the same thing as when we attribute a property to or deny it of that individual. And though this position is somewhat vague, perhaps, it doesn't seem to me that it has to be identical with the Frege-Russellian position. It might, if given a sharp formulation, be defended when the Frege-Russellian position was rejected. All it says in itself is that somehow saying of an object that it exists is different from ascribing a property to it, in the ordinary sense of 'property.' Although this is vague, it has an intuitive appeal independent of the doctrine that existence should not be ascribed to individuals at all.

7. Notice that the argument that even pretended names for sense-data must be allowable, as described in Lecture I, can be used to supplement Moore's argument about sense-data. See note 21 and accompanying text.

the only genuine individuals. But for me the point can be more general. Though this particular piece of chalk in fact exists, it might not have, as Moore argued against Russell even in the case of sense-data.[8]

Russell argues that if existence applied to individuals, it would be absolutely impossible for the property not to apply, and that this is characteristic of a mistake. Moore's argument would appear to show that something is wrong here. Now, in the Frege-Russellian apparatus of quantification theory itself there would seem to be a natural definition of saying that x exists:

$$10.\ E(x)$$

Namely that there is a y which is x:

$$11.\ (\exists y)(y = x)$$

(where x and y are both variables ranging over objects). So it is hard for me to see that they can consistently maintain that existence is only a second-level concept (in the Fregean terminology) and does not apply to individuals.

But what about the argument that it is "absolutely impossible for it not to apply"? Of course, it is the case that for every x there is a y such that $y = x$:

$$12.\ (x)(\exists y)(y = x)$$

In other words, 'for every x, x exists' will be a theorem of quantification theory, and so it will presumably be necessary. At any rate, I agree with Russell that it couldn't have been the case that "something" didn't exist. Things are not of two kinds, existers and nonexisters.

(12) is thus a necessary truth. The necessity of (12) can be written as:

$$13.\ \Box\ (x)E(x)$$

---

8. If one thought that some objects (say, numbers) *did* have necessary existence, this would be a significant fact about each such object and should imply *a fortriori* that the object exists.

However, this should not be confused with 'everything has necessary existence.'

$$14.\ (x)\ \Box E(x)$$

Of course it is this second step that Moore denies when he points out that under certain circumstances this piece of chalk, say, or even this Russellian sense-datum, wouldn't have existed. Thus, existence should not be confused with such a predicate as self-identity, where not only the analogue of (13), but the analogue of (14) does hold. (Here I assume that something is self-identical even with respect to counterfactual situations where it would not exist.)

There are, however, modal systems proposed in the literature, in which one could deduce (14) from (13), indeed could deduce $(x)\ \Box P(x)$ from $\Box(x)P(x)$. Actually, there are some in which the two statements can be shown to be equivalent, that is, that the converse holds.[9] I discussed in Kripke (1963) what I believe here to be the fallacy in any such derivation; I won't discuss it again here. Another source of confusion may lie in the following observation. Suppose that, to follow the line we have been taking, to express a proposition about Moses, and to use the name 'Moses' as a name, there has got to be an object referred to, namely, Moses. Then how could 'Moses does not exist' ever have been true? For if there hadn't been a Moses, we wouldn't have been able to use this name; we wouldn't have been able to say so; and perhaps even the proposition that Moses doesn't exist itself wouldn't have existed. To take the

---

9. Prior (1956) showed that this inference holds in S5. Applied to existence, this would imply that only a constant domain semantics is possible in quantified S5, which seems to me not to be true, though I myself was taken in by this view in my first paper on quantified modal logic (Kripke 1959).

other line is to say that it would have been around, but inexpressible by or inaccessible to us.[10]

Let's suppose that if there had been no way to speak of Moses in that way, one couldn't have said that Moses did not exist, or even that the proposition wouldn't have existed. So how could it be true of any possible world that Moses wouldn't have existed in it? We couldn't have said so if he didn't. This, it seems to me, is a fundamental confusion. One should not identify what people *would* have been able to say in hypothetical circumstances, if they had obtained, with what *we* can say, *of* these circumstances, perhaps knowing that they don't obtain. It is the latter which is the case here. We do have the name 'Moses,' and it is part of our language, whether it would have been part of our language in other circumstances or not. And we can say, of certain hypothetical circumstances, that in those circumstances Moses wouldn't have existed; and that our statement 'Moses exists' is false of those circumstances, even though we might go on to say that under some such circumstances, had they obtained, one would not have been able to say what we can say of those circumstances. (Perhaps, if one wishes to take this view of propositions, the proposition wouldn't have existed to be expressed, let alone that we couldn't have expressed it.) Still, we *do* have this form of language and we *do* have this proposition. In just the same way we can say, of certain hypothetical circumstances, that life might not have existed in the

---

10. I was assuming here that what does not exist (ever) cannot be named. So, had Moses never existed, he couldn't have been named. But perhaps this isn't always so, if the hypothetical nonexistent entity could be specified. Perhaps the person that would have existed, had a particular sperm united with a particular egg and had there been normal development (no splitting into two identical twins, or damage to the union, enough to say one doesn't have the same person), is completely specified and could be given a name, even if the union did not actually occur. Similarly, one might speak of the statue that would have, but in fact was not, formed from particular clay in a particular way. Maybe this entity could be named also. (Here I am supposing that the sperm and the egg, or the lump of clay, actually exist.)

universe, and so there would have been no one to express anything. As for the question which propositions would have existed under these circumstances, I might leave this here for someone else to answer.

Anyway, one should not identify what people would have said *in* certain circumstances, *had* those circumstances obtained, with what we would say *of* certain circumstances, knowing or believing that these circumstances *don't* obtain. The two are different. So one shouldn't think that if instead of a universally quantified variable as in (14), one had used a name such as 'Moses,' then 'Moses exists' has got to be necessary, because of some such consideration. (This would get something close to (14) back, by a different confusion.)

Perhaps more interesting is the question of modal statements using names from fiction, such as 'Is it possible that Sherlock Holmes would have existed?' For example, one modal logician, talking about this very question while setting up his apparatus, speaks of the problem that though Sherlock Holmes does not exist, in other states of affairs he would have existed, and then talks about the problems of modal logic which thus arise.

My present position, of course, must be in disagreement with any such view of fictional names. The modal logician was trying to make the point that there might have been objects other than the ones which actually exist, but he shouldn't, in my opinion, have made it this way, though the point is otherwise, of course, correct. I mean, is it correct to say there might have been a Sherlock Holmes? Of course, there might have been a great detective who did exploits precisely as described. That is true. Of course, on my view, if statements containing 'Sherlock Holmes' express pretended propositions—or rather, pretend to express propositions—one can't speak of a pretended proposition as possible.

But why shouldn't one say that such a situation is a situation in which Sherlock Holmes would have existed? I mean, someone might have performed these exploits, and Conan Doyle might have written of him. So why not suppose, as is being done by the modal logician, that Sherlock Holmes is some possible but not actual entity?

Certainly someone might have done the deeds ascribed to Holmes in the stories. Indeed, many *actual* people in the appropriate time period (late nineteenth century to early twentieth century) might have done them. But none of these people would have been Sherlock Holmes.

The fact is that in introducing the name we make 'Sherlock Holmes' name a particular man who would have done certain things, not just any old man who did these things. It will be part of this story of Sherlock Holmes that, of course, he may not be uniquely called forth to do these things. Holmes might remark to Watson that, had he not been such a great detective, his brother Mycroft would have been equally good, but not wishing to be a rival, he went into another field. So 'Sherlock Holmes' doesn't designate the person— any old person—who did these things: it is supposed to be a name of a unique man. And there is no unique man being named, nor is there any possible man being named here.

Part of the source of confusion lies in what I have inveighed against in *N&N*: the identification of metaphysics with epistemology. Here I am talking about what we would say of various counterfactual situations. A source of the belief that Sherlock Holmes *might have* existed might be that after all it could turn out that Sherlock Homes *really does* exist. Well, it could turn out: that is an epistemic question. If it turns out that Sherlock Holmes really exists, then my supposition that the name is fictional is wrong. Maybe Doyle was writing newspaper or magazine articles or a series of historical reports[11] and didn't at all realize that anyone would take him to be writing stories. If so, I am wrong, and I am under a mistaken impression that there are no such genuine propositions as that Sherlock Holmes lived on Baker Street. I am simply mistaken about this. It may turn out for all I know that I *have* made such a mistake. But if I am not mistaken as to the status of these alleged propositions—and I don't think there are any such propositions—then I am also not mistaken in saying that one cannot say that they would have been true of a certain hypothetical world: for there are no propositions to be true of this hypothetical world. There is only, in place of the possibility of such propositions, the possibility of the existentially quantified story—the possibility that there should have been a person *x* who did these things. This, however, is not the possibility that Sherlock Holmes existed. So, at any rate, my view goes.

I didn't give the reference to the modal logician with whom I usually agree (and I should say in fairness that the point he wished to make could have been made without using a name from fiction). The logician was Saul Kripke, in "Semantical Considerations on Modal Logic" (Kripke 1963). He does inform me that he was skeptical of this particular statement even when he read the printer's proof, but thought there would have to be too many changes made in proof to take it out.[12]

---

11. Better, his friend or acquaintance, Dr. Watson, gave them to him to be published. (According to *Wikipedia*, not quite all Holmes stories are narrated by Watson. Although narration by Watson is the typical case, there is some first-person narration by Holmes himself, and some third-person narration, including some longer works unknown to even Holmes or Watson.)

12. What he (I) wanted to say was simply that there might have been things other than what actually exist. Also, some of the things that actually exist might not have. And the same thing applies to all possible worlds. So a "variable domain" semantics for modal logic is required. The point about Sherlock Holmes and my real intent is mentioned in *N&N* (Kripke 1972/1980: 158).

More surprisingly, I wish to apply this to certain predicates also. Especially prominent in discourse about non-existence, and supposedly unproblematic in the way that the case of naming was not, is the case of various empty predicates, of which a very common example is 'unicorn.' Other ones are 'dragon,' 'chimera' and so on—various mythical types of species. It is commonly supposed, and not even argued, that though there are in fact no unicorns, first, it could of course turn out that there are unicorns, that we are mistaken; I agree with that, though not on the picture usually supposed; second, that it is possible that there should have been unicorns: under certain definitely specifiable circumstances there *would* have been unicorns. This I reject: that there should have been unicorns, on my doctrine, does not describe any definite possibility.

There are two things to sort out here. First, the epistemic question, under what circumstances it would turn out that, contrary to what we think, there are unicorns. Second, given that we are right in our supposition that there are no unicorns, *could* there have been unicorns? Under what circumstances *would* there have been unicorns? And here I reject the common doctrine just as I did in the case of Sherlock Holmes.

Is it possible that there should have been unicorns? The conventional picture, usually presupposed rather than stated, is this. Let's suppose that in the myth all we are told about unicorns is that they look like white horses and they have a certain horn sticking out in a certain way. I guess we are told a few other things too, but it would be sufficient to leave out the extra things: it wouldn't really change the picture. Let's also suppose, as is presumably the case, that there never have been any unicorns. Then at first it might appear that there would have been unicorns, counterfactually, precisely if there would have been animals which look like a horse and have one horn.

Now, remember here we are supposing that there are no unicorns. What is the role of the term 'unicorn' in the legend of the unicorn? First, the important thing to note is that unicorns are a kind of animal—a hypothetical, mythical species. It would then be, by the Pretense Principle, part at least of the pretense of the myth, that there is a species which I can describe and identify as looking just so.

The logic of such a species term can perhaps be derived by comparison with the logic of the name of an appropriate actual species. One might similarly identify a tiger as "a large carnivorous quadrupedal cat-like animal, tawny-yellow in color with blackish transverse stripes and light belly" (*The Shorter Oxford English Dictionary*). Here let's take 'cat-like' to mean just 'looking like a big cat' rather than actually 'feline,' or 'in the cat family,' because it certainly wasn't part of the original definition of 'tiger' anyway that it belongs to any particular biological family; the biologists had to investigate whether it really belongs to the family it looks like: they couldn't just do this by ratiocination. One might suppose, as Mill seemed to do, that a tiger can be defined simply as any animal satisfying these criteria. Well, it can't. Why?

First, it is not necessarily the case that any animal that looks like this is a tiger. On the contrary, if there were a reptile which looked just like this, but had a different internal structure (in fact, David Lewis told me that there is something called a marsupial tiger), the animals of the species would not be tigers no matter how good they were as dead ringers for tigers, just as fool's gold, no matter how much it looks like gold, is not gold, because it has a different internal structure. Tigers are a natural kind, and to be a tiger one must be of that natural kind. So it is not the case that any animal looking like this need be a tiger by definition. Of course, we may hope or believe that no such perfect ringers exist. The less they do, the easier it is to identify species by their appearances. But there is no logical requirement that this be the case—certainly if only surface appearance is in question.

Second, it is not the case that it is part of the definition of the term 'tiger' that tigers have got to look like that. By this I don't mean merely that there can be freakish tigers which have only three legs. I mean also that—though the discovery would no doubt be bizarre and unexpected—we could discover that we were wrong about the surface characteristics which we thought identified tigers. Perhaps in the regions of the world where tigers exist there is a curious kind of refraction or reflection, or something or other in the air—of course, it is very unlikely, and hard to flesh out in realistic, scientific terms—which makes us see their legs double, so they may have only two legs rather than four. If so, we would not have discovered that there were in fact no tigers, but rather that, contrary to what we thought, tigers were bipeds, not quadrupeds. Similarly, if we discovered that there were some optical illusion prevailing and gold were really green rather than yellow—it just *looked* yellow in the regions in which it was found—we would not conclude that there was no gold: we would rather conclude that, contrary to what we thought, gold was not characteristically yellow, but rather characteristically green.[13]

These considerations have led me to conclude that a natural kind term in ordinary discourse has some function like that of a proper name—that it refers to the things of the same substance or species or whatever is in question, as 'the kind of animal given by this original sample.' One does have certain surface characteristics

13. I recall reading a couple of references that attribute to Putnam the idea that only impurities in the gold around us produce the apparent yellow color, and that chemically pure gold would not be yellow. Epistemically, this is certainly a possibility, and an elegant way of bringing out the point that 'gold is yellow' is not *a priori* certain. However, as far as I have been able to ascertain, chemically pure gold is in fact yellow.

which one will believe that, in the absence of further investigation, will identify further instances of the kind. However, (*a*) one may turn out to be wrong about which surface characteristics are really relevant. (There may be boundary conditions here. It may be that if we are very far wrong one shouldn't say 'Tigers have turned out to be chemical elements rather than animals' but rather 'Tigers don't really exist.' There are other conditions too, but one certainly can be wrong in very important and gross ways.) (*b*) Any animals which aren't of the same kind—that is, don't resemble, say in internal structure, the things in this original sample—are not tigers no matter how much they resemble tigers, and no matter how difficult it was, when one originally saw tigers, to distinguish them from these other animals. It is true that we wouldn't know what the internal structure was; so we can't say that the term 'tiger' *means* 'having such and such biological structure on the inside,' because we don't know it. That is a matter for biological investigation. But we can say that to be a tiger you have to be the same kind of animal as this. That is briefly and very roughly stated.[14]

The term 'unicorn' or 'dragon,' being a pretended name of a species, should, I think, presumably have the very same logic. Only one is here pretending that a species has been identified rather than actually identifying it. Given that this is so, first, let's suppose that I am right in my supposition that both the term 'unicorn' and the term 'dragon' are mythical, that a species has not been genuinely identified. If so, can one say that under certain circumstances there might have been unicorns? Well, of course there might have been animals

---

14. Since I gave these lectures it has been pointed out to me that the males of some (unusual) species may resemble the females very little, so this might have to be taken into account. Considerations of evolutionary ancestry may also be relevant. No doubt the situation is simpler with chemical natural kinds than is the biological case. (In the latter case, I also use the term 'species' rather loosely.)

There is a parallel discussion of this topic in *N&N*, Lecture III.

that *looked* like white horses and had one horn. But that isn't sufficient. Take the case of tigers. 'Might there have been tigers in the Antarctic?' A situation in which there are animals *looking* like tigers in the Antarctic is not necessarily a situation in which there would have been *tigers* in the Antarctic. There has got to be another condition that these hypothetical animals must satisfy to be tigers, that is, that they are of the same species, have the same internal structure. Now one would like to add the same condition here: not only should they look like unicorns but they should *be* unicorns, have the same internal structure. Unfortunately, the story just doesn't tell us what the internal structure of a unicorn is supposed to be, and therefore it hasn't told us which hypothetical animal to look for in another possible world. Many hypothetical beasts might have satisfied all the descriptions in the story that unicorns or dragons satisfy. Dragons are perhaps an even clearer case than unicorns: one wouldn't suppose them to have any particular internal structure, though one might attribute the internal structure of a horse to a unicorn. One can't say that *all* the various hypothetical species that resemble dragons are dragons, because dragons are supposed to be a single natural kind—this I am supposing is part of the story. (And so are unicorns.) Yet, we are not told which. Therefore, one cannot say of any particular possible world that it would have contained dragons.[15]

It might even be part of the story that there are animals which look just like unicorns—'fool's unicorns' they are called—and are often taken for them. Certainly, that could be consistently added to the story. As far as I am aware, it is not part of the story that there is only one species which looks like this. Certainly it need not be.

15. I should not be taken to be saying that it is impossible that there should have been dragons or that there should have been unicorns (like composite primes, or, according to me, water, that is not H_2O). Rather, that the counterfactual possibility is ill-defined, given that there are no dragons or unicorns.

Second, what about the epistemic situation? Of course, it could turn out that there actually were unicorns, but under what circumstances would this be so? One might say, 'Well, look, as long as there turned out to be animals that look like this, that is when it would turn out that there would be unicorns.' Well, notice what I said about the parallel case of Sherlock Holmes: that though there might be a great detective who did all the things in the story, that would not prove that the story was true reportage rather than fiction. On the contrary, the saying 'The characters in this story are fictional and any resemblance to persons living or dead is purely coincidental' may be true. Similarly, one may say here, if the term 'unicorn' has a logic similar to that of 'tiger' except that it occurs in fiction, that 'The *species* in this myth is fictional and any resemblance to actual species extant or extinct is purely coincidental.' The clause would make just as much sense here as in the case of a particular. If it had been the case that someone invented the story of the unicorn and simply spun it out of his head with no connection to any actual species, one could not say—even though his mythical animal precisely matched something in the real world—that he was talking about that kind of animal, any more than one could make the analogous claim in the case of Sherlock Holmes. This would be even more clear if he had gone on to talk about fool's unicorns, for then the actual animal would match both the unicorns and the fool's unicorns, and one couldn't say which of the two animals he was in fact talking about.

One could, of course, introduce a term, say '*schmunicorn*,' just to be a predicate meaning 'member of the species of animals, if there is in fact a unique one, which is identified by the following surface characteristics: having one horn and looking like a white horse.' If so, then something is a *schmunicorn* if, and only if, a species with these surface characteristics exists. But I think that this is probably not even the way the term 'unicorn' was used by the medievals, who took the term seriously. They probably did believe that there was only one species that looked like this. But I think they wouldn't[16] have held this to be analytic of the term 'unicorn' in the sense that it could not turn out that there was some species other than the unicorn which looked just like this. On the contrary, suppose (I don't know if this is part of any myth) that Sir Galahad is supposed to have met a unicorn, and they really believed that this happened. A medieval would, I think, agree that if somewhere in some part of the world there is a species of animals other than that of which a specimen was met by Sir Galahad, but which looked like it, they would not be unicorns. If they would agree to that, this shows that they would not mean by the term 'unicorn' simply 'a member of a species which looks like this,' because they would acknowledge the epistemic possibility that it should turn out that there was another species, not the unicorn, which did have these surface characteristics.

They would also, I think, acknowledge that they could turn out to be mistaken in supposing that unicorns had only one horn. Perhaps it could turn out, I think they should acknowledge, that it has two horns, but the other one is so tiny and buried under the principal one that it wasn't noticed by any knight. And I think they should also acknowledge that in this case, even though there was another species of animal unknown to them in darkest Africa, which did have only one horn and looked like a horse (at least looked as much like a horse as a unicorn does), those were not unicorns. It turns out that the description that they applied to unicorns applies more accurately to these other animals, but these were not the animals with whom they thought the knights had all these famous encounters, even though they misdescribed them in a significant detail.[17]

---

16. Or *shouldn't*, given that they thought that unicorns were a natural kind.
17. Although I ascribe the belief in unicorns to medieval times, it may have been even older and persisted longer.

If these are epistemic possibilities which could be acknowledged by the medievals, then the medieval does not mean by the term 'unicorn' 'the unique species identified by such and such surface characteristics.' He uses it, as he uses the term 'tiger,' with respect to a hypothetical sample that people have met, which they have taken to be identifiable by such and such surface characteristics. But the possibility of mistake exists in both directions, both in the possibility of ringers, fool's unicorns, and in the possibility that we've made some mistake in our description of the species itself.

If so, then, one cannot just say that any species which looks like this, if it exists, is the species of unicorns. Rather, if one wishes to use the term 'unicorn' as those who used it in the middle ages did—as those who spun the legends did—one must acknowledge that to prove that unicorns could have existed one must prove that this species that looks like the unicorn has some historical connection with the myth as we have found it. Of course, we might find it convenient to call such a species 'unicorns.' If we synthesized them in the laboratory we might call them 'unicorns'; but we shouldn't say that we have now made the very same animals that the medievals were talking about. We haven't.[18]

There are two things at issue here. First, given that there *are* no unicorns, that it *is* a myth, could there have been other circumstances under which there would have been? I argue no. Second, epistemically speaking, I of course acknowledge that it might turn out that there really are unicorns, but one shouldn't regard this question as simply a question about whether there is an animal

---

18. However, if the story of the unicorns were historically connected to some genuine and ordinary kind of animal (even one known to us today), and the mythical traits attributed to it gradually evolved, we would probably not say that it turned out that unicorns really existed after all. There are borderline cases, so one cannot give a hard-and-fast rule. But in the strong circumstances mentioned in the first sentence of this note, one would probably indeed deny that unicorns had really turned out to exist.

matching the description in the myth. That is not a sufficient condition even for there actually being unicorns.

Here one is tempted to say 'Look, you can't say, "Given that there are no unicorns, you can't say that there might have been unicorns"—you've just acknowledged that there might have turned out to be unicorns! And we know that there are no unicorns, so what possibility are we excluding here?' I won't answer this now. It is the same kind of question as the analogous question about Sherlock Holmes. If you say Sherlock Holmes does not exist, then if you are not excluding a possibility, what are you saying; what *are* you excluding here? But I will say this: one would be much less tempted to think that there might have been bandersnatches than that there might have been unicorns. For what are we told about bandersnatches? Here we are not told any surface characteristics, other than that the bandersnatch is frumious; and apparently a frumious animal is a very dangerous one, or anyway it should be shunned.[19] That is all the poem has told us about them. Here one doesn't think that there is any hypothetical animal: 'Given that there are no bandersnatches, under what circumstances would there have been bandersnatches?' It is altogether unclear because nothing has been said about what a bandersnatch would be. If it doesn't describe a species, one simply rejects the term altogether, rather than thinking that it could apply in various hypothetical circumstances. An important difference is that here one doesn't know what such a thing would even have looked like. It usually is a pretty good guide to being in a species, how something appears: if one is shown a picture of a tiger one thinks one can recognize them. That is because dead ringers are in fact very unlikely; and the better picture one has got the less likely one is going to be confused by a ringer. But other than that the

---

19. The reference is of course to Lewis Carroll's poem "Jabberwocky."

situation is really not so different. Here too it could turn out that, contrary to what we thought, there really were bandersnatches. I once read a hypothetical story about Lewis Carroll in which it turned out that that was the case. Contrary to what we thought, he was writing a straightforward report about bandersnatches. (Actually I didn't read a story; it was a comic strip.) At any rate this could turn out to have been the case. Suppose we had asked him and he said he was quite surprised that people thought he was talking about imaginary animals here; why, he himself used to be warned to avoid them when he walked through the park as a child, and that is what they were always called in his little region, though apparently the term has passed out of usage.

So one could discover that, contrary to what we thought, bandersnatches are real. And of course we express the fact that such a discovery hasn't occurred by saying that bandersnatches aren't real, that there are no bandersnatches, and so on. That is not to say, given that there are no bandersnatches—that the bandersnatch is imaginary— that we can then speak of the circumstances under which there *would have been* bandersnatches. The term 'bandersnatch' is just a pretended name of a species; it doesn't really *designate a species*, and once one knows that this is the case, one cannot say under what circumstances there would have been bandersnatches.

I think that the case of such a term as 'dragon' or 'unicorn' is no different, though we are told something more about them, something which would perhaps be enough to identify them uniquely if there were such. Because there will be no actual ringers around, we can then investigate their internal structure to distinguish them from hypothetical ringers that might have existed in other possible worlds. But if this trail of investigation leads to the conclusion that the term 'unicorn' or 'dragon' is merely pretense, then no hypothetical species has been named. And the status of the predicate 'is a unicorn' should be precisely analogous to that of the hypothetical proper name 'Sherlock Holmes' in the detective story case, or (perhaps an example which might not be clear) to that of a hypothetical color, 'plagenta' say, which none of us has seen—and it is indescribable—but which occurs in such and such a story. Given that the storyteller is talking about nothing, one can't say under what circumstances something would have been colored plagenta. All these things are mere pretenses.

This being the time limit, as usual I have not said everything I should like to say. In fact, the main thing I thought I was going to talk about I didn't get to; I will get to it next time. I will introduce it now.

Before talking about the negative existential any further, there are various senses, I think at least two, in which it is true to say that Sherlock Holmes exists. And before talking about any way in which Sherlock Holmes doesn't exist, I should talk about the senses in which he *does*, the senses in which the statement 'There really is a Sherlock Holmes' is true.

November 13, 1973

Various people have found Russell's account of empty proper names, and in particular of proper names in fiction and mythology, objectionable. An example is in the collection of some of Russell's essays edited by Douglas Lackey. Lackey says:

> In this controversy [between Russell and Meinong] Russell has usually appeared to be an apostle of common sense while Meinong has appeared as a wild ontologizer hypostasizing entities at will. But Meinong's theory says that "Pegasus is a flying horse" is true, while Russell says that this assertion is false. The average man, if he knows his mythology, would probably agree with Meinong.
>
> (Russell 1973: 19)

This objection has been repeated by many people, and I believe it came up in the question period after the first of these lectures.[1] Richard Cartwright, for example, speaking about this in Cartwright (1960), says that surely it is true that 'Faffner had no fur' is a statement about Faffner; and similarly to say that Faffner isn't real is to make a statement about Faffner, despite its non-existence.

Hintikka goes even further. In a famous paper on Descartes (Hintikka 1962) he argues that the Cartesian *cogito*, *if* it is to be taken as a logical inference, would be fallacious; for the inference purports to infer 'I exist' from 'I think,' but Hamlet truly thought many things,

---

1. As far as I am aware, no record of the question periods has been preserved.

and yet Hamlet never existed. And I suppose 'I soliloquize; therefore, I exist' would be an even more fallacious inference on this account. Because of this, Hintikka thinks we must invent a presupposition-free logic in which from 'Fa,' 'There is an x such that Fx'—that is,

$$1. \ (\exists x)(Fx)$$

—doesn't follow, without the supplementary premise that a exists, represented as follows:

$$2. \ (\exists x)(x = a)$$

Here, after all, 'a' could be an empty name. Then 'Fa' shouldn't imply 'There is something which has F.' For example, 'Pegasus has wings' shouldn't imply 'There is something that has wings,' even if the conclusion is true, any more than 'Pegasus is a winged horse' should imply that there is a winged horse.

I am not going to discuss the merits of this kind of logic, or its utility for the general case of empty names. Such logics are now called "free logics," and they have a certain role in the literature. I think they are important, in fact, for making the philosophical point that if one treated names as singular terms instead of parsing them out via invented predicates as Quine does, one would not be forced to conclude that there is a winged horse, or that there is a god, without further ado, where the former conclusion is false and the latter controversial.[2]

---

2. In *Mathematical Logic*, Quine argues that from '$(x)(x$ exists)' one would be forced to conclude that 'God exists' and 'Pegasus exists,' if 'God' and 'Pegasus' are "primitive names." Hence he advocates eliminating such names and replacing them by corresponding predicates 'god x' and 'peg x.' Then one could define 'God' as '$\imath x$ god x,' and similarly for Pegasus. Quine rightly adds that the difficulty would not disappear if one denied that existence is a predicate (see Quine 1940: 150).

However, though formal systems of free logic may show that Quine's argument is not inevitable, on the other hand, Quine does show that one need not use such systems to get around the problems. One could use his device of invented predicates.

I do think they are useful for that purpose. But here I just want to discuss the merits of the particular argument that Hintikka gives.

What do we mean when we say that Hamlet thought many things? It seems clear that there *is* a sense in which the assertion is true. A pupil would receive a low mark if, on a true-false test, he marked 'Hamlet soliloquized' as 'false'. It would seem that in such a usage we count a statement involving a fictional name as true if it is true according to the appropriate story in which the fictional entity or fictional name appears. If so, such a statement might be interpreted simply as having the implicit qualifier, 'in the story'. Such a way of looking at things, and such a problem, is important for us—that is for me—as well as for Russell; because just as Russell might be faced with the objection that according to him the statements would be one and all false, so I might be faced with the objection that, while according to what I have said thus far they express pretended propositions, or merely pretend to express a proposition, in fact such statements are true.

It does seem, though, that when we make such a report on what is in the story, we are saying something which is in some sense a comment on what is in the story, and this could be shown by reference to the case where the fictional character appears in two contradictory stories, where there are two variant legends about that character. In that case one wouldn't just say 'Jones'—if Jones was the name of the legendary character—'was fond of beer': one would say 'In story *A* Jones is fond of beer, but in story *B*, not.' One would not say something without qualification in this case.

However, this is the exceptional case and normally this usage doesn't entirely depend on an explicit statement of what story is involved. One can get oneself, so to speak, into the spirit of the story, rather than explicitly stating that the story says 'Pegasus has wings' or 'Jones was fond of beer' or whatever. At any rate, it seems uncontestable that when one makes such a statement the general rule is that it counts as true if it is a true report of what is in the story. One can regard this as a form of ellipsis, or not, as one pleases.

Taking this as a special usage, then, 'Hamlet soliloquizes' is of course true because according to the appropriate story Hamlet does soliloquize. So does it follow that one can say that Hamlet soliloquizes, but Hamlet does not exist? And I am sure that according to the story Hamlet *thought* too, so maybe 'Hamlet thinks' does not imply 'Hamlet exists,' and this is an invalid form, as Hintikka says.

It seems to me that such a conclusion would be quite fallacious. If one wishes to take the premise in such a way that its truth conditions are given by what is said in the story, one must take the conclusion in the same sense. And so taken, the conclusion that Hamlet exists is of course true also, since according to the story there is a Hamlet; Hamlet does exist whether or not this is just a story, whether or not Hamlet exists outside the story. So it seems to me that Hintikka's argument establishes nothing against the *cogito* construed as an inference, as he puts it.

Nor would such arguments establish anything against Russell. If one wished to analyze 'Hamlet' as a definite description—let's say 'the melancholy Danish prince' (where it is assumed that every other Danish prince was jolly, perhaps a plausible assumption about that country)—then the Russellian analysis of 'Hamlet thought' or 'Hamlet soliloquized' will be 'There was a unique melancholy Danish prince, and every melancholy Danish prince thought' or 'soliloquized'—or what have you; and this also will be true according to the story.

One thing which I think is a source of confusion here is the tendency to take the conclusion in a different way from the way one takes the premise. The trouble is that there is—or at least at this stage there seems to be—only one way to take the premise. The premise 'Hamlet thinks' merely purports to express a proposition rather than really expressing one. And so one wouldn't ever take it as really expressing one; if taken as true, it must be interpreted within the story. Whereas the conclusion 'Hamlet exists' can be taken as about reality rather than about what is true according to the story, and so might be interpreted as false.

Second, the conclusion that Hamlet exists, taken as a statement with the truth conditions suggested, might appear to be trivial. That is, one might think 'Well, of course, *according to the story* everything mentioned in it automatically exists.' That isn't true. Just as in real life there can be fictional characters, imaginary things, mistakes about Vulcan, and so on, so there can be in a story. One can ask as a serious question about a story in literature, such as whether Macbeth's dagger really existed or was merely a phantasm of his mind (here, most would take the second view). One can similarly ask whether Hamlet really saw the ghost of his father, or whether there was no such ghost. This could even be a question debated by literary critics. They would be asking here what is true according to the story, and they would be asking a serious question. Suppose someone thought that Hamlet merely imagined that he saw a ghost. He might then say very seriously as a report on the story, 'Though Hamlet existed, the ghost of his father did not.' Someone else might take a contrary view. I would be inclined to say, as I think most would, that the ghost of Hamlet's father was real, though Macbeth's dagger was not.

In *Hamlet*, Hamlet asks the players to put on a play for the King, as you all know, called *The Murder of Gonzago*. Reporting on the story we should say that though Hamlet was a real person, there was no such person as Gonzago. For Gonzago here is merely a character, presumably, in a supposed famous *play*. There *does* exist a *play* called *The Murder of Gonzago*. Here notice the ambiguity between what one says according to the story, and what one would say according to real life. According to real life there is, as far as we know, no such play as *The Murder of Gonzago,* but according to the story there *is* such a play.[3]

If one takes everything in a single sense there will be no case here for saying that one can attach a simple positive property to a proper name, yet say in the same breath that that thing does not exist. There might be some other case for saying this, but examples from fiction do not constitute such a case. It is quite true that one shouldn't dismiss ordinary language here: someone who marked, according to some Russellian paradigm, 'Hamlet soliloquized' 'false' on an English test in school would get a bad grade justly, not a good one, and he shouldn't say that Russell's analysis shows that the statement is false. Russell's analysis is being misapplied here if it is taken to show that the statement is false. If one replaced 'Hamlet' by a definite description like 'the melancholy Danish prince' and even analyzed it in Russell's manner, the statement would be true, and not false, *as a report on what is in the story.*

So far, so good. Notice then that in this sense it is true, and not false, to say that Hamlet exists. And many authors have been mistaken about this. Cartwright (1960: 637) is similarly mistaken in his article, it seems to me, when he wishes to say in the same breath that Faffner lacked fur, but that Faffner didn't exist—as if these were two parallel statements about Faffner. They are statements of two different kinds.[4] One shouldn't combine them together and say that here we have an example of something that both didn't exist and had no fur—at least not on the basis of this kind of argument.

3. When I was about to give a version of these talks at UCLA, I phoned the English department and found a Shakespeare expert (whose name, unfortunately, I didn't preserve), who told me that in fact Gonzago was a real person (who was killed), though they know of no such play. But (now) I have been unable to verify this conclusively on the Internet, though there definitely was a House of Gonzaga (not Gonzago) of Italian noblemen. Regardless of the facts, I have let stand the assumption in the text that the play is a fictional play and Gonzago a fictional fictional character (for this terminology, see below).

4. In spite of my view that Cartwright is mistaken in this formulation, I at least (partly) agree with him later, when I advocate an ontology of fictional and mythological characters.

Are we home free here with respect to this kind of question? Are there any other kinds of positive-sounding statements, other than those interpreted within a story, which apparently use empty names? Other examples which might give us trouble are these. First kind of example: 'Hamlet was a fictional character.' Second kind of example: 'This literary critic admires Desdemona, and despises Iago'; 'The Greeks worshipped Zeus'; and so on. In the second case there appears to be a relational statement, with a real subject and an apparently empty name or names as objects.

What can we say about these examples? Neither of them seems to be analyzable according to the paradigm we just suggested, as reports on what is in a particular story, with their truth conditions being given by that story. The story doesn't say that Hamlet is a fictional character. On the contrary, this would be to misread the story. The story says that Gonzago is a fictional character; not that Hamlet is. A very poor student in school who got confused on this point might in a true-false test (I don't know if you have these awful things here in England) incorrectly mark 'Hamlet was a fictional character' 'true.' But that would be incorrect. He should mark that 'false,' and 'Gonzago is a fictional character' 'true,' if he wishes to report on what is in the story. So it seems to me that this kind of statement cannot be analyzed according to our paradigm. Similarly, of course, no story says that such and such literary critic admired Desdemona: I take that to be fairly obvious. That the literary critic did so is a fact *in rerum natura*.

How then are we to analyze these kinds of cases? Let me sketch some initial stabs that might be taken. First, one might say that to talk of fictional characters is only a sort of weird grammatical trick: 'Hamlet was a fictional person,' or (let's make it metalinguistic) '"Hamlet"—the name "Hamlet"—is the name of a fictional person,' really should be re-analyzed as: 'In fiction "Hamlet" was the name of a person.' This certainly has something to do with the concept of a fictional character, but it is hardly adequate for extended uses of such a terminology. Using more than one name, one can say for example (if one were crazy enough) 'Falstaff and Iago were two of the most charming fictional characters in literature.' One might reanalyze this as being about the names: '"Falstaff" and "Iago" were two fictional names in literature of charming characters in their respective stories.' By some amount of torturing one can get things to work. Even if someone makes an existential statement of the form 'There is a fictional character who married his mother, though there is no fictional character who married his great-aunt' (if that is true), one might be able to torture this around into a statement about the stories themselves and the terms that occur in them.

One can think of more and more complicated analyses which might produce apparently equivalent statements. Such analyses should not of course suppose that every fictional character is in fact named, because that need not be so. There may be a fictional character who is unnamed in his own story. But it does seem as if, taken straightforwardly, such statements appear to be about a realm of entities which we call fictional characters.

More moves have been made in the literature about the second problem, apparently intensional verbs: I won't go into them all. But let me mention some of the main directions of attack which can be or have been used.

What happens when we say that a certain literary critic admired Desdemona? There are various lines that have been taken. One line is suggested by a remark of Quine's. Quine suggests the following: 'I want a sloop,' in the opaque sense, means 'I wish myself to have a sloop,' that is, to be a sloop owner; 'I want a sloop,' in the transparent sense, means 'There is a sloop that I want.'

Only in the latter sense is 'want' a relative term, relating people to sloops. In the other or opaque sense it is not a relative term relating people to anything at all, concrete or abstract, real or ideal. It is a shortcut verb whose use is set forth by 'I wish myself to have a sloop,' wherein 'have' and 'sloop' continue to rate as general terms as usual but merely happen to have an opaque construction 'wish to' overlying them. This point needs to be noticed by philosophers worried over the nature of objects of desire.

(Quine 1960: 155–56)

I don't know how general Quine means this suggestion to be. He applies it to those philosophers who are worried over the question of objects of desire. There was a considerable discussion in the literature, of course, especially in the Meinongian or German "pre-phenomenological" literature,[5] on intentional objects of this sort, involving the postulation of objects of desire when someone wants something which doesn't exist.

What is the analysis here? First, 'I want a . . .' should be analyzed as something like 'I wish myself to have a . . .,' or just 'I wish to have a . . .'; or, to make it expressly a propositional attitude, which is what Quine really wants, 'I wish that I had a . . . .' So 'I want a sloop' should be analyzed according to this paradigm as 'I wish that I had a sloop.'

There are then two analyses of this. One is 'I wish that there is an x such that x is a sloop and I have x':

1. I wish that $(\exists x)(\text{Sloop}(x) \wedge \text{I have } x)$

That is, one scope for the existential quantifier which corresponds to the indefinite article 'a' in 'I want a sloop.' The other is 'There is an x such that x is a sloop and I wish that I have x':

2. $(\exists x)(\text{Sloop}(x) \wedge \text{I wish that I have } x)$

---

5. I mean figures such as Bolzano, Brentano, and the like, as well as Meinong, who are sometimes said to be in the "background of phenomenology." I confess to knowing very little about them.

This is the familiar distinction of scope which was introduced into logic by Russell, for both definite and indefinite descriptions (Russell 1905), and it comes out pretty clearly here. On the first interpretation it is not required that there is any particular sloop that I want, or even that I want something that exists in any sense at all. It is merely that I wish that there be a sloop which I have. To put things in Quine's terminology (not in *Word and Object*, from which I am quoting, but in his 1956 paper "Quantifiers and Propositional Attitudes"), on the first interpretation all that I wish is relief from slooplessness.

I don't know (and indeed doubt) that Quine would have recommended this as a line of solution to the present problem. More clearly intended that way is a comment by Church:

> According to the Fregean theory of meaning which we are advocating 'Schliemann sought the site of Troy' asserts a certain relation as holding, not between Schliemann and the site of Troy (for Schliemann might have sought the site of Troy, though Troy had been a purely fabulous city, and its site had not existed), but between Schliemann and a certain concept, namely that of the site of Troy.[6] This is, however, not to say that 'Schliemann sought the site of Troy' means the same as 'Schliemann sought the concept of the site of Troy.' On the contrary, the first sentence asserts the holding of a certain relation between Schliemann and the concept of the site of Troy, and is true; but the second sentence asserts the holding of a like relation between Schliemann and the concept of the concept of the site of Troy, and is very likely false. The relation holding between Schliemann and the concept of the

---

6. For those of you who are familiar with Fregean terminology, Church doesn't use the term 'concept' as Frege does; in his usage, the concept of the site of Troy is the Fregean sense of the phrase 'site of Troy.'

site of Troy is not quite of having sought, or at least it is misleading to call it that—in view of the way in which the verb *to
seek* is commonly used in English.

(Church 1956: 8, note 20)

On this kind of paradigm, when someone says 'The Greeks worshipped Zeus,' his statement asserts a relation between the Greeks
and the sense of the expression 'Zeus.' It is then to be analyzed similarly to the way Frege analyzes intensional contexts, which are more
explicitly given by propositional attitudes. In fact, in the case of the
verb 'to seek,' which Church gives here, one can replace the verb
by one which really takes the form of a propositional attitude:
'Schliemann strove that he should find the site of Troy' or something like that might be in the analysis.[7] But Church would apply this
paradigm anyway, whether such an analysis could be given or not.

Church also regards 'the site of Troy' as intensional ('oblique'),
so that if the site of Troy happened to be the site of some other city,
one could not substitute the other term.[8] Perhaps even more relevant to our discussion is the following example: 'Lady Hamilton
was like Aphrodite in beauty' (Church 1956: 27, note 71). He also
says that "'The myth of *Pegasus*,' and 'The search by Ponce de Leon
for the *fountain of youth*' are to be explained as exhibiting oblique
occurrences of the italicized constituent name" (1956: 9, note 22). In
Church (1951: 111–12, note 14) he uses 'I am thinking of Pegasus,'
'Ponce de Leon searched for the fountain of youth,' and 'Barbara
Villiers was less chaste than Diana' as examples more readily han-
dled by a Fregean theory than by Russell's theory of descriptions.[9]

---

7. If it is done this way, a Russellian analysis would be possible. Or, for that matter, a Quinean
analysis in the sense of Quine (1956).
8. This example is indeed intensional for the reason given. However, as we shall see, this is not
the general case.
9. My thanks to Anthony Anderson for suggesting this reference.

These examples directly relate to 'the Greeks worshipped Zeus' and the like.

What about these suggestions? Actually they have a common feature in that they both take the verb here as intensional, though Quine of course doesn't use a Fregean sense and reference apparatus, while Church does. As I said, I am quite unsure how general Quine intended this theory to be, whether it was supposed to be an explanation for all putative intensional object statements of this kind, or only of some particular ones about desire: he does remark that it should be taken notice of by those philosophers who are interested in objects of desire.

Let me make an initial comment on Quine first. If you really wish *only* for release from slooplessness, and there is no particular sloop that you want, then you can say this colloquially by adding some such phrase as 'any old sloop' afterwards: 'I want a sloop, any old sloop.' That will disambiguate the statement.[10] It seems to me clear that such a disambiguation is not so happy in parallel cases involving admiration and worship.

Suppose one uses an explicit indefinite description instead of an empty name: 'The Greeks worshipped a god.' Can they have worshipped "a god, any old god"? 'Such and such a literary critic admired a fictional woman.' *Any old* fictional woman? It *may* be so! But probably not. Even if he did admire any old fictional woman that doesn't mean that he merely desired release from fictional womanlessness, whatever that may mean. (*Actual* womanlessness, maybe.)[11] The

---

10. That is, if all you want is "relief from slooplessness." One might want a sloop with further specifications, even though one might not want any particular sloop. And then a grammatical illusion of a particular object might be created—e. g., "I want a sloop. *It* must be about *x* feet long." See Partee (1970).

11. In any case, in the analysis I have replaced 'admire' by 'desire,' simply to make things intelligible. There is no need to make such a replacement, nor to think that Quine would do so, or even use 'desire' in the analysis of 'admire.'

statement that the literary critic admired "any old fictional woman" would still be a statement of the form 'For every x, if x is a fictional woman, he admired x,' not a statement of propositional attitude followed by an internal existential quantifier as in the sloop case (see (1) above).

In fact, it seems difficult or impossible to apply Quine's analysis here. Another difficulty in applying it arises in this case, too: how are we to parse out such verbs as 'admire' and 'worship' in terms of a propositional attitude followed by an appropriate 'that' clause? At any rate, I don't know how to do it, and I am inclined to think it impossible, just because if it could so be parsed out, then there would be an ambiguity of interpretation for 'the critic admired a fictional woman' or 'the Greeks worshipped a pagan god.' But there seems to me to be no such ambiguity in these cases. To say that the Greeks worshipped a pagan god is to say that there is a specific pagan god that they worshipped; not, so to speak, something about pagan godhood in general. Even in the case of 'wants,' which can be analyzed in this way, it may be that a certain pagan wanted, say, to meet a god; and though this might mean that he wanted to meet a god, any old god—that is he wanted to be free from "lack of meeting gods"—it might also mean that there is a particular god that he wanted to meet. This second interpretation seems to me to make sense: the answer to the question which god he wanted to meet might be 'Zeus.' So an analysis of this reading can't be given by Quine's paradigm. As I already emphasized, I don't know how general Quine intended his remarks to be.

More obviously intended to be applicable to the present problem is Church's analysis. For example, a term like 'worship' would relate a subject to a Fregean *Sinn*. So, when you say that the pagan worships Zeus, the term 'worships' expresses a relation between him and the Fregean *Sinn* of the term 'Zeus.' As Church says, this is not to say that he worshipped the Fregean *Sinn*: that would be to express a relation between the pagan and the Fregean *Sinn* of a Fregean *Sinn*.

What about this analysis? Applying it here seems to me to be beset by various difficulties. First, it implies that the verb 'worship' is intensional, in the sense of not being subject to ordinary substitutivity of identity. But this seems to me not to be so. And similarly for 'admires.' Suppose Schmidt admired Hitler. If Hitler was the most murderous man in history, then it seems to me that Schmidt did admire the most murderous man in history. And it does not seem to me that the latter statement is ambiguous as between an intensional, or opaque, and a transparent one. There is not one sense in which he did admire the most murderous man in history and another in which he didn't. If he himself would deny that Hitler can be so characterized, then it is true that he didn't admire Hitler *as* the most murderous man in history. But it still is true that he admired the most murderous man in history. He wouldn't have so described him, but it seems to me that there isn't a sense in which this statement is false. It is true of course that perhaps he wouldn't *say* 'I admire the most murderous man in history,' and it is true that Hitler isn't being admired *qua* the most murderous man in history, if Schmidt thinks that he is a pacific, saintly, gentle character. But still, it seems to me that it is nevertheless unambiguously true that Schmidt can be accused of admiring the most murderous man in history. This objection may not hold for all the contexts Church would classify as oblique (including some mentioned above). But it seems to me probably to be the case for 'admires' and for 'worships.' If there really is anyone to admire or worship, substitutivity of identity applies. If the Romans worshipped Caligula, and Caligula was a mere mortal, then the Romans did worship a mere mortal. Perhaps they didn't think that he was a mere mortal. They wouldn't have worshipped him if they had thought he was a mere mortal. But still they after all worshipped a mere mortal.

Now even when 'worships' is followed by an apparently empty name we can make such substitutions. Suppose the Greeks worshipped Zeus, and Zeus is the tenth god mentioned by Livy. Then the Greeks did worship the tenth god mentioned by Livy. (Of course, they weren't particularly thinking of him as the tenth god mentioned by Livy when they did so.)

If the sense-reference analysis of this example were correct, such an inference would be out-and-out fallacious. But rather than its being out-and-out fallacious it seems to me to be correct. If we were concerned with a relation between a thing and a Fregean *Sinn*, the Fregean *Sinn* of the phrase following the verb, then the inference will be incorrect because, of course, 'Zeus' and 'the tenth Greek god mentioned by Livy' have two different Fregean senses: so the inference should be fallacious. But it isn't fallacious, and even if someone thought there was a sense—which I don't think there is in the case of some intensional verbs—under which substitution doesn't hold, one should try and apply the theory to the case where substitutivity *does* hold, although it seems that the object doesn't exist, as in 'Zeus is the tenth Greek god mentioned by Livy.'

There are really two problems being rolled into one here. One is the apparent non-existence of the object; the other is intensionality in the sense of failure of substitutivity. In this case they don't seem to me in any clear way to go together. Let me say what I think the true account of these matters should be.

Everything seems to me to favor attributing to ordinary language an ontology of fictional entities, such as fictional characters, with respect to which ordinary language has the full apparatus of quantification and identity. I say 'full apparatus'—well, we may not be able to make every possible statement; but both notions, at any rate, apply to these entities. 'Ah,' so it is said, 'so you agree with Meinong after all! There *are* entities which have only a secondary kind of existence.' No, I don't mean that. I mean that there are certain fictional characters in the actual world, that these entities actually exist.

'What do you mean by this?' Let me give an example. I once had the following conversation with Professor Harry Frankfurt. I was explaining to him something about the Bible. Many of you may know the famous pagan god, Moloch. (We are told, at any rate, that there is such a famous pagan god.) It is often assumed popularly, and so a straightforward reading of the Bible would go, that the Israelites are being reprimanded again and again for human sacrifices to this vicious pagan god, Moloch, whom they worshipped when they went astray in an idolatrous mood. Lots of biblical scholarship, doubtful that there was any such god in a pagan pantheon, has adopted one of the following two theories. (Well, these two I have seen; maybe there are more.)

One is that 'Moloch' is a misvocalization of the Hebrew word 'melech' for 'king'; that the sacrifices to Moloch were actually sacrifices to the king. 'The king' here, according to some, was probably just another name for the same monotheistic god that the Hebrews worshipped, that is for Jahweh. There was no pagan god involved at all. The name later came to be misvocalized and misconstrued as if there were such a pagan god.

The second theory is that 'Moloch' was the name, not of the god worshipped, but of the kind of sacrifice; that a particular kind of human sacrifice was called a 'Moloch sacrifice,' and the preposition mistranslated as 'to' should be rendered as something like 'as': 'He sacrificed his son *as* a Moloch' (just as in the Hebrew bible certain types of sacrifices were called 'burnt offerings,' 'sin offerings,' and so on). This view is that of Otto Eissfeldt.[12] Note that, on his view, 'Moloch' is not the name of a god at all.

On either of these views, we can conclude there was no such god as Moloch, and that the assumption that there *was* such a god is based on a mistake. Professor Frankfurt jokingly replied, "Of course there was not such a god. You don't believe in pagan deities, do you?"

What is going on here? It is clear that when we ask 'Was there such a god as Moloch?' we are asking a question about the world: 'Is there such a legendary character?' And the question can have an affirmative or a negative answer. It is not the same question as the question whether there really is such a god, in the *other* sense of 'god,' where there has to be a real supernatural being worthy of worship, or something of the kind, to back the term up.

So my view is that ordinary language quantifies over a realm of fictional or mythological entities. They don't exist, so to speak, automatically: that is, they are not Meinongian in the sense that whatever is an object of thought exists in some second-class sense. On the contrary, it is an empirical question whether there was such and such a fictional character. Was there a fictional or legendary character who married his grandmother? (There, of course, *was* a famous one who married his mother.) If there was, this will be true in virtue of appropriate works of fiction or legend having been written, or at least told orally, or something of the kind. If there is such a fictional work, then there is such a fictional character.

12. See Eissfeldt (1935). The final clause of the title means 'the end of the god Moloch.' Eissfeldt's theory (derived from Punic inscriptions that he thought used 'Moloch' in the sense in question) was very popular in things I read at the time of these lectures. More recent commentaries I have seen do not seem to accept it. Obviously the truth or falsity of the theory is irrelevant to the conceptual point, which requires only that the theory makes sense.

Novels and dramas do not exist in some weak Meinong-land: there actually have been many novels in the ordinary world. True, they are not as concrete as the particular manuscripts, book-tokens, and performances that create them. On my view, to write a novel is, ordinarily, to create several fictional characters, as Twain, by writing *Huckleberry Finn*, brought both a novel and a fictional character into being. It is not that fictional characters exist in one sense but not in another. The fictional character Huckleberry Finn definitely exists, just as the novel does: I would withdraw the statement only if my impression that there was any real novel was mistaken. Thus, their existence is not like that of numbers, abstract entities which are said to necessarily exist, independently of empirical facts.

A name such as 'Hamlet' might have been said to designate nothing, or only to pretend to designate something; one also now speaks of it as designating a fictional character. There is such a fictional character, if an appropriate work of fiction has been written. Thus there is such a fictional character as Hamlet, and there is no such fictional or mythical god as Moloch, if the theories I have been mentioning are correct. 'Moloch' would be a name like 'Vulcan,' mistakenly thought to designate a mythical god, just as 'Vulcan' was mistakenly thought to designate a planet. So there can be empty names of fictional or mythical characters. Such statements then as 'The Greeks worshipped Zeus' can of course be taken as expressing an ordinary two-place relation between the Greeks and a certain pagan god. And similarly, 'Leavis admired Tess' would express a relation between a critic and a certain fictional woman.

We can also have a pretense about a fictional character, as in the case of Gonzago. Only in the play *Hamlet*, or let's suppose so, it is said that there is such a play as *The Murder of Gonzago*. If so, we can say that there is no such fictional character as Gonzago. Here we are not reporting on what is in the play, because the play does say that there is such a fictional character as Gonzago. We are speaking now about the real world. There is in fact no such fictional character as Gonzago, though the play pretends that there is. There is, however, a *fictional* fictional character called 'Gonzago' (see, however, note 3).[13] This is true in virtue of the existence of the play *Hamlet*. And just as I have said, in the case of Sherlock Holmes, that there is no possible entity which we call 'Sherlock Holmes,' so there is no possible fictional character called 'Gonzago.' For though many plays with the title *The Murder of Gonzago* might have been written, one cannot say which of them would have been *this* play *The Murder of Gonzago*, or which of them would have had *this* fictional character Gonzago in it. I hope this is not confusing.

A fictional character, then, is an abstract entity. It exists in virtue of more concrete activities of telling stories, writing plays, writing novels, and so on, under criteria which I won't try to state precisely, but which should have their own obvious intuitive character. It is an abstract entity which exists in virtue of more concrete activities the same way that a nation is an abstract entity which exists in virtue of concrete relations between people. A particular statement about a nation might be analyzable out in virtue of a more complicated one about the activities of people, or it might not: it might be hard, or maybe, because of problems of open texture, impossible to do so. But, at any rate, the statement about the nation is true in virtue of, and solely in virtue of, the activities of the people.[14] I hold the same thing to be true of fictional characters. Thus they are not Meinongian entities which, so to speak, automatically exist. They exist in

---

13. And though there is no such play as *The Murder of Gonzago*, there is such a fictional play.
14. Another problem pointed out to me (by Rogers Albritton) is that the people in the nation must think of themselves as in that nation when doing various things as citizens, so that the activities of the individual people are apparently not describable independently of the notion of a nation.

virtue of certain activities of people just as nations do. Of course, a fictional person isn't a person. There aren't in addition to the people who actually lived in London in the nineteenth century fictional people who did so.

But here there is a confusing double usage of predication which can get us into trouble. Well why? Let me give an example. There are two types of predications we can make about Hamlet. Taking 'Hamlet' to refer to a fictional character rather than to be an empty name, one can say 'Hamlet has been discussed by many critics,' or 'Hamlet was melancholy'—from which we can existentially infer that there was a fictional character who was discussed by many critics and was melancholy, given that Hamlet is a fictional character.

These two predicates should be taken in different senses. The second predicate, 'is melancholy,' has attached to it the implicit qualifier *fictionally*, or *in the story*. Whereas of course the first, 'is discussed by many critics,' does not have this implicit qualifier. Let's take the statement 'Hamlet was a fictional character.' That is not true in the work of fiction itself. Using predicates according to their use in fiction—that is, according to the rule which applies a predicate to a fictional character if that fictional character is so described in the appropriate work of fiction—we should conclude that Hamlet was not a fictional character. In fact, paradoxical as it may sound, in this sense no fictional person is a fictional person. For (virtually) no fictional person is said in his own work of fiction to be a fictional person.[15] But applying the predicate on the level of reality—that is, so to speak, straight—one should say that Hamlet *was* a fictional person, and that every fictional person is a fictional person.

---

15. However, complications do occur, leading to my parenthetical qualification. See, for example, "Enoch Soames" by Max Beerbohm and *The Comforters* by Muriel Spark. In some other version of the present lectures, I discussed at least these works. But I won't give away any plots here.

One will get quite confused if one doesn't get these two different kinds of predications straight. One may be inclined to conclude that in addition to there being people who live on Baker Street, there are also fictional people who live on Baker Street. Well, yes there are, but the fictional people who live on Baker Street are not said to live on Baker Street in the same sense that real people are said to live on Baker Street. In the one case one is applying the predicate straight; in the other case one is applying it according to a rule in which it would be true if the people are so described in the story. And ambiguities can arise here because of these two uses of the predicate.

Consider an example. Suppose I write a story about a character whom I will call 'Frank Franklin.' I may have other characters besides this fictional character in the story. Let F. R. Leavis be a character in the story also, and let Frank Franklin be admired by F. R. Leavis: it is part of the story that F. R. Leavis admires him. Then Frank Franklin is a fictional character who is admired by F. R. Leavis, in the same sense in which Hamlet was a fictional character who was stabbed by Laertes. But F. R. Leavis may read the story, and not admire the character at all. If so, we should say, using the phrase 'admired by F. R. Leavis' in the straight sense, that Frank Franklin is a fictional character who is not admired by F. R. Leavis, although in the earlier sense Frank Franklin *is* so admired.

So the fact of the ambiguity should be recognized. A name in a story may refer to a real person, that is, really refer to a person. For example, as I have said, we could have a fictional story about Napoleon. In that case there is no such fictional character as Napoleon; it is rather that a real person is being written about, here in fiction. In fiction it may be said, as in one story about Napoleon, that Napoleon lived his whole life in the time of the Bourbons. I hope that some of you may know the story by Stephen Vincent Benét, "The Curfew Tolls." In this story Napoleon is pre-dated to an earlier era.

He lives his entire life under the French monarchy, and spends his life in idle dreams of what his military glory could have been.

Probably if you just hear the statement 'Napoleon lived and died in the time of the French monarchy' you will take it as out-and-out false, because it is not about a fictional character—it is about the real Napoleon. So here, since this is a fictional story about a real person, we must add an explicit qualification 'according to the story' to ascribe the predicate to Napoleon. Or at least, the context must make it clear that this is what we are doing.

I hope you have a rough idea, then, of the kind of ontology I have in mind for a straightforward analysis of our ordinary discourse. This is not to say that a so-called scientific language[16] necessarily has to include these entities. Perhaps one can get along just with quantification over people and the works that they write, or even merely the concrete copies of these works, and so on. This is a matter which I don't intend to discuss. But, for the most straightforward construal of our ordinary discourse, I think we do have this kind of ontology.

It should not be regarded as a Meinongian ontology. It is a fact that certain fictional and mythological characters exist, just as it is a fact that certain people exist. No fictional characters would exist if people had never told fiction; no pagan gods would ever have existed if there had never been paganism; and so on. It is a contingent empirical fact that such entities do in fact exist: they exist in virtue of the concrete activities of people.

One can raise identity questions between fictional characters as between anything else. First, of a more straightforward and trivial kind, 'Was Zeus the Greek god whom that man worshipped?' The answer may be yes, and it may be no. If that man worshipped Zeus,

---

16. I was thinking of philosophers, of whom Quine is a prime example, who think that 'scientific language' can reject much of ordinary discourse. It isn't my attitude here.

and Zeus was the god another man worshipped, then he worshipped the same god the other man worshipped. Substitutivity of identity should hold here; it should not fail, as it would fail if the object of the verb 'worship' were the Fregean sense of the phrase which follows it, as Church thought.

One can ask again—and this is perhaps a different kind of question—whether Zeus and Jupiter were the same god—the same pagan god—or merely analogous gods in two different pantheons. I don't know what the answer is. But it seems to me that, though there might be some purposes for which one should just straightforwardly insist that there are two different fictional gods here, for those purposes for which this is a serious question the answer will be given in terms of tracing the legend historically. If, say, the Roman legend arose out of the Greek one, and the name was simply changed from Greek to Latin at a certain point, or gradually changed, then these are the same god rather than two different gods with analogous roles in the two different pantheons. If, on the other hand, the two pantheons had independent origins, then these *are* two different gods with analogous roles in different pantheons.

So identity questions here seem to me to make sense, and their answer is usually the subject of historical research which traces whether one character is the same as another.[17]

---

17. Usually the answer to identity questions between fictional (or mythological) characters is obvious. Of course Hamlet is not Macbeth, etc. As to the idea in much philosophical literature that there is a basic demand for a "criterion of identity" for a type of object before it can be discussed intelligibly, I reject this idea and do not think that an intelligible account of it as a general demand about all kinds of entities can be given. But I cannot elaborate on this remark here. (I do so in my unpublished lectures, *Time and Identity*).

Perhaps I should say that in the discussion section of my earlier paper on this issue (Kripke 2011b), Quine asked as to what the "criterion of identity" was for fictional characters, and later gave fictional characters as a paradigm case where there is no criterion of identity; see, "Second General Discussion Session" (Dummett et al. 1974).

Finally, at any rate, my view gives another sense in which it is true rather than false that Hamlet exists. At least, one should say 'There really is such a fictional character as Hamlet.' Such a fictional character really exists, whereas there really is no such fictional character as Gonzago, and no such fictional character as Moloch—these two for different reasons. Gonzago is really a *fictional* fictional character, but not a real fictional character. Moloch, perhaps—at least originally as in the Bible—isn't even a *fictional* fictional character: the whole idea that there is such a fictional character, or such a pagan god, a legendary object, is simply based on a confusion (at least it is based on a confusion if either of the two theories that I mentioned to you is correct).

So in this sense, instead of saying that the name 'Hamlet' designates nothing, we say that it really does designate something, something that really exists in the real world, not in a Meinongian, shadowy land. When we talk in this way, we use names such as 'Hamlet' to designate abstract but quite real entities, and can raise existence questions about whether there are such entities with given properties.

Another issue, however, is this: a fictional character, created in a given corpus, may later appear in other works. For example, Sherlock Holmes appears in various films. One should think of this case as similar to the appearance of Napoleon or George Washington in fictional works. I have spoken of the permissibility of predicating properties of fictional characters according to the story in which they appear. However, if a fictional character appears in an extended corpus, then one must specify the non-original work, unless it is obvious from the context. Thus, one can say, 'In the Basil Rathbone–Nigel Bruce Sherlock Holmes movies, Dr. Watson was unintelligent, though this was not so in the original stories.'

Lecture IV

November 20, 1973

Last time what I was trying to do was to give some account of the senses in which such a statement as 'Hamlet exists' might be taken as true rather than false. Today I am going to talk about applications elsewhere of some of the notions used in that account, but perhaps I should first briefly review them.

The main thing I talked about in the last lecture was the ontology of fictional characters. From some comments that I have heard in the intervening period, I am not sure that everything I have said has been precisely understood. For one thing, in spite of my best efforts to insist on the contrary, some people seem to have supposed that I am talking about a weaker sense of existence, or some kind of shadowy realm, or perhaps about existing "in fiction," or "in imagination," or something like that.

When I speak of the ontology of fictional characters, I don't want to say any of these things, whatever their merits. One might use the sentence 'Hamlet exists in fiction' to mean 'fictionally, Hamlet exists.' But in that sense, of course, it is also true that, fictionally, Hamlet is not a fictional character. These are the within-the-story kind of reports. In this kind of usage, 'Hamlet exists' really shouldn't be regarded as reporting on a separate realm of existence, but as a form of ellipsis in which a statement ϕ is used with truth conditions appropriate to 'the story says that ϕ,' or 'the story implies in some sense that ϕ.' In that sense Hamlet exists, but also in that sense Hamlet isn't a fictional character—in that sense 'Hamlet is a real person' is true.

But when I speak of the ontology of fictional characters I am trying to give a report on the ordinary usage, first, of certain quantifications that we can make—such as 'Large numbers of people in English fiction have been in love,' or 'There are fictional characters from the seventeenth century who are discussed by no literary critics today' (if that is true, and even with the very assiduous nature of literary critics it probably is true); and also of various kinds of object statements that we make, such as that a certain literary critic admires Desdemona, or the like. These statements are not true in fiction, or in any special realm: they are *actually* true, and they relate people to a kind of entity whose existence is actually being claimed as an empirical claim. There might have been, of course, no fictional characters at all, had no fictional works been created. The only way in which one might say that they have a different kind of existence from anything else would be parallel to the way nations have a different kind of existence from people, the way in which more abstract entities exist, as opposed to more concrete ones. If this is regarded as a different sense of existence, then the existence of fictional characters is different too, because they exist merely in virtue of the activities of people.

One thing which I think has caused confusion is the use of the word 'real' here, where I contrast a fictional person with a "real" person. If the fictional person isn't "real," then after all there must be a weaker kind of existence involved. I don't wish to make that kind of use of the word 'real,' or that kind of comparison, when I speak of fictional characters. When I do this, a more appropriate comparison would be with the contrast between 'real duck' and 'toy duck.' Of course there are differences as well as similarities. But just as a toy duck isn't a real duck—though of course that doesn't mean that the toy duck doesn't really exist[1]—so I want to say that a fictional person

---

1. This remark is probably an anticipation of what I call the "toy-duck fallacy" in Kripke (2011c).

isn't a 'real' person—though that isn't to say that, in and of himself, he doesn't really exist, or isn't real, in the sense of 'doesn't exist.' On the contrary, just as there can be real toy ducks, and perhaps things that are taken to be toy ducks which aren't in fact even *toy* ducks, so Hamlet is a real fictional character, whereas Gonzago and Moloch are neither of them real fictional characters, whatever other kinds of entities they may be. There isn't really such a fictional or legendary entity as Moloch, if the views about Moloch which I described last time are true; and there really isn't any such fictional character as Gonzago, though I guess there is really such a fictional fictional character. If, just now, I introduce a name 'Snazzo' for an alleged fictional fictional character, of course I have just made it up, and there really isn't such a fictional fictional character, nor such a fictional character either. It is in this sense that I wish to talk about real entities and fictional ones.

The introduction of the ontology of fictional characters is in some sense a derivative or extended use of language, at least on the picture that I was presenting. When one originally introduces the term 'Hamlet' there is merely a pretense of reference, and there is no referent—period. But then we find a referent by the ontology of fictional characters, so that we can say 'the story refers to a fictional character,' if we like, or 'the sentence in the story refers to a fictional character,' or we can say, when we talk about Hamlet, that we refer to a fictional character.

One shouldn't confuse the extended use in which the term 'Hamlet' really has a referent (not just "in the story") with the original picture according to which 'Hamlet' would have no referent—according to which Hamlet would not exist. And when one makes the contrast between, as I might call them, real entities and fictional entities, one should think of things as follows. First, there are kinds of entities, such as people, that would be around in the absence of any fictional works. There are also kinds of entities (let's call them kinds of entities K) that are themselves the product of fiction (or mythology). When a story is written about alleged entities of the kind K, then we speak of "fictional entities of kind K," or just "fictional Ks"—for example, fictional people, fictional ducks, or what have you, but there are also fictional elves, dragons, bandersnatches, and so on. In the latter case, the fictional entities are more or less motivated by a resemblance to real kinds, though (as we have seen) the story may give no specification of what they would be. We can refer to particular fictional entities such as 'Hamlet' or 'Frodo,' as well as to particular fictional kinds, such as hobbits and bandersnatches.

The fictional process can also be iterated: a story can itself write about the writing of stories, and a play can speak of a play being put on. That is how we get *fictional* fictional characters, and so on. So when we speak of real entities as opposed to fictional entities, we don't speak of entities which have a more or less shadowy kind of existence—that is not what is in question. It is like, in some respects, 'real duck' and 'toy duck'; it satisfies the paradigm. The entities which one calls 'real entities' are the ones which one could talk about before one told any stories. When one imitates this and tells stories, then one has fictional entities of the same kind. Then fictional fictional entities arrive, when a story itself talks about stories. And so on *ad infinitum*, though usually the iteration doesn't go too far.

I spoke of language as supplying a referent. A referent, of course, need not be supplied if the work of fiction or the story is about ordinary entities of the primary kind like, say, people. If this is so, then when one uses the name 'Napoleon' in a story about Napoleon or 'George Washington' in the story of his chopping down the cherry tree, one need not say that the name here refers to a fictional character; one can say that it refers to Napoleon, or to George Washington, himself.

Just as in the case of an ordinary person that one can admire for some of his (real) qualities and not for others, so I could admire Napoleon as portrayed in the story, but not in real life, or vice versa. (And of course, actually, I could admire him for some of his qualities in the story, or in real life, but not others.)

We have seen that in the case of fictional characters, predicates can be read in two ways, either as what is true of them according to the fictional work in which they appear, or in an "out-and-out" sense. Remember the fictional character Frank Franklin admired by F. R. Leavis in one sense but not the other. A good example came up last time in the question period. 'When was Frankenstein's monster created?' If the predicate is read out-and-out, with no qualifier 'fictionally,' it was created in whatever year the novel was originally written. If the predicate is applied with the qualifier 'fictionally' in front of it, then Frankenstein's monster was created whenever the novel says that Frankenstein created it, which may well be in a different year.

In the case of Napoleon, obviously the preferred reading of any predicates (provided they make sense that way)[2] are the predicates that apply to him historically, the out-and-out reading. If one has a story in mind, and the predication is according to the story, one had better say so explicitly.

What I wanted to talk about this time was the application of these matters to problems of perceptual verbs and objects of sight, as opposed to the question of reference. I feel here, more strongly than in the case of fictional characters, that more work needs to be done, and that the whole matter is very complicated. Nevertheless, my idea is that certain analogues of what I have been saying about

---

2. If, say, Napoleon says something to Prince Andrei in *War and Peace*, plainly this does not have a historical interpretation, since Prince Andrei is a fictional character.

the different types of predication that might be involved in talk of fiction has some application to certain aspects of the philosophical dispute about perception (in particular, one aspect of Austin's criticism of some prior work of Ayer).

This dispute has had various features. First, it has been mixed in, in a way that no one would contemplate in the case of fiction, with problems of epistemology. What things do we know indubitably? Does the external world exist? And so on. I am not concerned with that whole complex of problems. I don't want to be concerned with any epistemological problem here, and if a philosopher who says, for example, that we never directly perceive a table is concerned with an epistemological problem, and means that the existence of the table is subject to doubt in the way that something else is not, he may or may not be correct, but he isn't talking about the same problem that I want to talk about.[3]

The problem I do want to discuss, probably too briefly, is the kind of problem which Moore, for example, discusses when he introduces sense-data. (He, of course, is not well-known as an epistemological skeptic.) Moore says:

> I saw a patch of a particular whitish colour [actually what he is looking at is an envelope], having a certain size, and a certain shape, a shape with rather sharp angles or corners and bounded by fairly straight lines. These things: this patch of a whitish

---

3. In the discussion below, I generally defend John Austin in at least one aspect of his dispute with A. J. Ayer. However, he appears in *Sense and Sensibilia* to think that he has refuted traditional epistemological skepticism and shown the arguments for it to be based on linguistic confusion. I don't think this, nor do I think that his arguments show that we cannot speak of visual impressions (or auditory impressions, etc.). There is clearly something that is the same if my eyes were presented with the same irradiations when I am not seeing the scene I actually see, and this is the same visual impression. Moreover, though I have presented this in terms of visual irradiations and the like, the concept itself is clear enough without such a scientific explanation.

colour, and its size and shape I did actually see. And I propose to call these things, the colour and size and shape, *sense-data*, things *given* or presented by the senses—given, in this case, by my sense of sight. Many philosophers have called these things which I call sense-data, *sensations*. They would say, for instance, that that particular patch of colour was a sensation. But it seems to me that the term 'sensation' is liable to be misleading. We should certainly say that I *had* a sensation, when I saw that colour. But when we say that I *had* a sensation, what we mean is, I think, that I had the experience which consisted in my *seeing* the colour.

(Moore 1953: 30; emphasis in text; note omitted)[4]

And Moore then goes on to say that he wants to talk about, not what we *have*, but what we *see*.

This is very important. Some people who have entered into these problems have talked about them as if the question at issue were the legitimacy of talk about having a visual impression, say, or having a certain experience, as if that could be described in and of itself. I myself, though this is probably hardly relevant to anything I am discussing here, have very little doubt of the legitimacy of talking about having a visual impression. It doesn't seem to me to be a doubtful question at all, and I get puzzled that others could doubt this. But whatever the answer to this question may be, it should be separated from the question of whether these visual impressions, or some other kind of special entity called a 'sense-datum' or whatever, is that which we really *see* (see note 3).

Moore just wants to give a quite ordinary-language argument for the objects of sight being something special, because he goes on to

---

4. Moore states in his preface that this is a printing of lectures actually delivered in the winter of 1910–11, so that in some respects his views have changed.

conclude that the sense-data can't be material objects, or parts of the surfaces of material objects, on the grounds that when I see this patch, I may see, for example, a trapezoidal patch, when the envelope is rectangular; and each of us from his own position sees a different shaped patch. Therefore the patch is not the envelope, for the envelope has only one shape and we each see a different shape. These are the kinds of arguments used.

It is just this kind of argument that I want to consider, in particular a well-known dispute between Ayer and Austin about this in Austin (1962) and Ayer (1940, 1967, and 1969). Ayer had written (1940: 19ff) that the verb 'to see' (actually, he uses 'perceive') has two "quite ordinary" senses. In one sense of 'see' the thing seen must exist, but need not have the qualities it appears to have. In another sense of 'see' the object seen need not exist (*in any sense at all*), but *must* have the qualities it appears to have. Obvious apparent cases of Ayer's second sense of 'see' would be, for example, the patient who "sees" pink rats in DTs,[5] or (in the auditory analogy) "hears" voices.[6]

We must eventually consider such cases, but I am more concerned with other examples that Ayer actually gives and Austin discusses. One example is seeing a star in the sky (Ayer 1940: 22–23). Clearly in one of Ayer's senses of 'see' what one sees is a huge astronomical object. This is the sense where what one sees must exist but need not have the qualities it appears to have. But one also "sees" (and this is supposed to be Ayer's second sense) a small speck in the sky (no bigger than a sixpence). Here the thing seen

---

5. Actually, Austin explicitly mentions this case before his denial that Ayer's second sense of 'see' or 'perceive' is to be found in ordinary language. See Austin (1962: 49).

6. A psychiatrist on the faculty of Oxford once told me a true story about a psychiatric colleague of his who was hearing voices. He said to her, "Well, what would you say about a patient who was hearing such voices?," and she replied, "Oh, that he had schizophrenia or a related delusion—but these are *real* voices."

need not exist in any sense at all, but must have the qualities that it appears to have. We will come back to this case, since for us it will be a crucial one.

As against Ayer's view, Austin has said several things, but the main point is that he denies that one of Ayer's two senses of 'see' is to be found in ordinary language at all. Namely, he denies that there is any sense of 'see' or 'perceive,' or whatever, in which the object seen need not exist *in any sense at all*, but must have the qualities it appears to have.[7] He emphasizes Ayer's use of the italicized phrase and wonders indeed what Ayer could mean. He asks,

> It is in fact very hard to understand how Ayer could ever have thought he was characterizing a *single* sense of 'see' by this conjunction of conditions. For how could one possibly say, in the same breath, 'It must really have the qualities it seems to have,' and 'It may not exist'? *What* must have the qualities it seems to have?
>
> (Austin 1962: 96, note 1; emphasis in text)

In a note he discusses the following example:

> What about seeing ghosts? Well, if I say that cousin Josephine once saw a ghost, even if I go on to say I don't 'believe in' ghosts, whatever that means, I can't say that ghosts don't exist *in any sense at all*. For there was, in *some* sense, this ghost that Josephine saw.

---

7. But note that for Austin's view to be viable, we have to allow for objects that once existed, but no longer exist. This is clear in the case of the existence of the stars, since we do see stars that have since gone out of existence. Austin himself does not make this clear.

The same holds for Ayer, in one of the senses of 'see' he postulates, where the object of sight must exist (again, the star).

As I have already remarked (Lecture I, note 6), to my ear 'Napoleon no longer exists' sounds fine, but the simple 'Napoleon does not exist' sounds rather odd, as if 'Napoleon' were an empty name.

> If I do want to insist that ghosts don't exist *in any sense at all*, I can't
> afford to admit that people ever see them—I shall have to say that
> they think they do, that they seem to see them, or what not.
>
> (Austin 1962: 95, note 1; emphasis in text)

Presumably, he will say similar things in the cases of the pink rats and the voices.

Discussing another similar example Ayer gives, where someone who has double vision says he sees two pieces of paper in front of him (Ayer 1940: 20–21), Austin takes a somewhat different view. He says that, though this statement can be said to mean something which is true *in these circumstances*, it doesn't introduce a different sense of 'see': rather, the statement isn't true if we take 'see' in its ordinary literal sense. 'See' is being used *faute de mieux* in very special circumstances in which it isn't really appropriate, though we do understand what is meant (Austin 1962: 89–91).

Another example Austin gives, which is supposed to be an analogue, is this:

> I might say, while visiting the zoo, 'That is a lion,' pointing to one
> of the animals. I might also say, pointing to a photograph in my
> album, 'That is a lion.' Does this show that the word 'lion' has *two
> senses*—one meaning an animal, the other a picture of an animal?
> Plainly not. In order (in this case) to cut down verbiage, I may
> use in one situation words primarily appropriate to the other;
> and no problem arises provided the circumstances are known.
>
> (Austin 1962: 91)

I want to say a little bit more about this example, because it is used by all subsequent authors in a way I don't like. Ayer mentions it in one of his replies to Austin, and says that it shows how 'is' need not always be the 'is' of identity, as it seems to be in 'that is a lion' (Ayer 1967: 137; quoted below). But it seems to me to be fairly plain that the example is being misinterpreted if 'that' is being taken to refer to a picture of an animal. Can one say, pointing at the picture, 'That is a lion, and I'll put it in my pocket'? I think one can't, and the reason is that 'that' doesn't refer to the picture—it refers to the animal depicted in the picture. And so one *shouldn't* say 'that is a lion and I'll put it in my pocket.' If I am right, then 'that' is literally a lion, in precisely the sense that the thing in the zoo is. If I say 'That is my cousin Herbie,' I don't really mean 'That is a picture of my cousin Herbie': I am showing who, in the picture, is my cousin Herbie. (And notice that I may be pointing him out among other people in the picture.) It seems to me that both Austin and people writing replies to him don't acknowledge this: I don't know why.[8]

This issue about what kind of 'is' is being used here, and what kind of 'that,' can get more important later. Austin, when he speaks about the problem of the speck, says that the answer simply is that in that case the speck *is* a star, or the star *is* a speck (1962: 99). Why should one speak of two different senses of 'see' here, or even two different kinds of object? He gives several examples:

But the proper explanation of the linguistic facts is not this at all; it is simply that what we 'perceive' can be described, identified, classified, characterized, named in many different ways. If I am asked 'What did you kick?,' I might answer 'I kicked a piece of painted wood,' or I might say 'I kicked Jones's front door'; both of these answers might well be correct; but should we say for that reason that 'kick' is used in them in different senses? Obviously not. What I kicked—in just one 'sense,' the ordinary one—could be described as a piece of painted wood, *or* identified as Jones's front door; the piece of wood in question *was* Jones's front door.

8. If we are not dealing with a picture, but with a painting of a lion, there may be no real lion being depicted. Here too when we say 'That is a lion,' we may be referring to a fictional lion, analogously to a fictional character in a story.

Similarly, I may say 'I see a silvery speck' or 'I see a huge star'; what I see—in the single, ordinary 'sense' this word has—can be described as a silvery speck, or identified as a very large star; for the speck in question *is* a very large star.

(Austin 1962: 98)

Austin gives several other examples in the same vein. I will quote just one more of these:

'I saw an insignificant-looking man in black trousers.' 'I saw Hitler.' Two different senses of 'saw'? Of course not.

(Austin 1962: 99)

So the same object is being described in two different ways; and here one and the same object is both a speck out there on the horizon and also a star. The examples I have quoted certainly seem to imply that the 'is' is that of identity, and as I said, there are many others in the same vein that I have not quoted. But there remain certain points to be dealt with. First, we have to see how he is to deal with Ayer's claim that the star and the speck cannot be the same, because we ascribe properties to them that are not only quite different sounding (as in the Hitler case), but are actually incompatible: the star is enormous but the speck is tiny. Moreover, Austin adds a note that seems incompatible with the assumption that when we say that the speck is a star, the 'is' is that of identity. He says:

It doesn't follow, of course, that we could properly say, 'That very large star is a speck.' I might say, 'That white dot on the horizon is my house,' but this would not license the conclusion that I live in a white dot.

(Austin 1962: 98, note)

But if the 'is' were the 'is' of identity, of course it would be a symmetric relation: if that speck is the star, then that star is the speck. And if the 'is' were the 'is' of identity, of course, it *would* license the conclusion that I live in a white dot. So perhaps some other kind of 'is' is involved here.

In the subsequent literature that I have seen, both defenders and critics seem to agree that the 'is' here can't be the 'is' of identity. Ayer says, as against Austin, that the 'is' can't be the 'is' of identity, as is shown by this example about a white dot, and also by the fact that, after all, the speck is no bigger than a sixpence (I guess there isn't a sixpence anymore is there? At least I haven't seen one around), whereas the star is many times bigger than the earth: they have incompatible properties, so how could they be identical? And various people have defended Austin, for example Warnock (1971). But even Warnock warned that Austin shouldn't really be taken as saying that the 'is' here is the 'is' of identity. If Warnock is right, one cannot really regard his remarks as totally a defense of Austin, since, as we have noted, in so many of his supposedly parallel examples the 'is' involved plainly is the 'is' of identity.

Well, if one can speak of the speck and the star, then, after all, there are either two entities or one. If they are not identical, what else is the speck if not the star? This actually seems to me to be a difficult problem. Here is what Warnock says about it:

> It is not that the star simply *is* a speck, but rather that a speck is what it visually *appears as*, when looked at in these conditions, with the naked eye, here and now.
>
> (1971: 4; emphasis in original)

Well, that is true: the star does appear as a speck. But still, is the speck a star? It is true, of course, that we can say 'the star appears as a speck,' but not 'the speck appears as a star.' But that doesn't show, in and of itself, that these are two different entities, any more than the fact (I hope this example is equally well-known over here) that 'Superman masquerades as Clark Kent' can be true, and 'Clark Kent masquerades as Superman' false. Superman is his real identity: he is just masquerading as an ordinary, mild-mannered reporter. So, Superman "appears as" Clark Kent in a sense in which Clark Kent doesn't "appear as" Superman: that is true. But that doesn't show that Clark Kent isn't Superman: it just shows that 'a appears as b' is a sort of intensional, opaque relation here that an entity can have to itself.

If the speck isn't the star, what, after all, *is* it? Ayer suggests this: first, he says:

> [W]e must not be too quick to assume that the 'is' is the 'is' of identity. This comes out clearly in such instances as that of pointing to a photograph and saying 'That is my Uncle James' or pointing to a map and saying 'Those are the Pyrenees.'
>
> (1967: 137)

This is really Austin's example again (though Ayer does not mention it), and my own view of the matter is the same. Of course I mean that the man in the picture is my Uncle James, not that the photograph is, in some bizarre sense of 'is,' my Uncle James. That of course would *not* be the 'is' of identity; but no such moral should be drawn. Again, if one points to a map and says 'Those are the Pyrenees,' it is the mountains represented, of course, which are the Pyrenees, not that the map is. (Or perhaps what is bothering Ayer is that neither Uncle James nor the Pyrenees is really within one's vision, but this too is not relevant.) He goes on:

> The case of the speck's being a star is more complicated because there are not two objects, as in the case of the photograph or

map. To treat the speck as a representation of the star would be to insinuate a theory of perception, rather than to analyze ordinary usage. For common sense, there is only one object, the star. The puzzle then arises that the properties ascribed to it by us under one appellation are incompatible with those ascribed to it under another. This looks like an infringement of the law of identity, until it is realized that, in talking of the speck, we are not referring to an object which is identical to the star, but only to the way the star appears to us. [What does that mean? S.K.] If we go on to treat such appearances as objects in their own right, which we are not bound but may be entitled to do, we cannot consistently identify them with the things of which they *are* appearances.

(Austin 1967: 137; emphasis added)

Here, I guess, he is saying that the speck is an appearance, or the way the star appears. That actually seems to me to infringe Leibniz's law. The speck, after all, is out there on the horizon; but the way the thing appears, whatever kind of entity that may be, isn't out there on the horizon.

So everyone seems to agree, both critics and defenders of Austin, that the 'is' in 'the speck is the star' can't be the 'is' of identity. In his rejoinder to Ayer, Forguson says that it is very strange that Ayer should have ever taken Austin to think that it was the 'is' of identity (see Forguson 1969). To me, it is obvious that the analogies given by Austin (say, the Hitler case mentioned above) would be misleading and irrelevant if the 'is' were *not* the 'is' of identity. And, if they think that the speck and the star are different objects, they had better give a better account than I am able to figure out of what the two different objects are.

How can one get a better view of this kind of problem? I think there can be a sort of analogy with the case of fiction and mythology.

Let me discuss first the cases involving hallucinations or delusions and come back to the star and the speck later. A suggestion might be this: one can attribute to language—when and if it extends the use of the verb 'see' to allow an object even when there is no physical object there—the recognition of a special kind of thing called 'the hallucinatory object,' which is seen. This must be done, as with Austin's ghosts, if one wishes to maintain his view that if one describes someone as seeing something, the sight must have an object. Similarly, the DTs patient who sees pink rats sees some hallucinatory objects. They can be described as pink rats, even though they are not real animals, by the same sort of convention that one can predicate of a fictional character its attributes in the story. In this usage, Macbeth saw a dagger, though it was a hallucinatory dagger. The dagger is not his visual impression: it is a special kind of entity, just as perhaps Austin might have meant to imply about seeing ghosts.[9]

Given this suggestion (and this, it seems to me, agrees with usage), of course the question whether there really is a given hallucinatory object is an empirical question, like that of whether there really is a certain fictional character. Suppose someone comes in and says she is having some kind of DTs, and that she sees a dagger in front of her. You can say 'There isn't any such hallucinatory dagger: she is simply lying,' if she in fact did lie, and is only pretending to have the DTs. Perhaps one might say that there never would have been hallucinatory rhinoceroses, if there haven't ever been—if no one has ever had such a hallucination.

9. Talking of the DTs sufferer, Austin says that "in exceptional situations ordinary forms of words may be used without being *meant* in quite the ordinary way; our saying of the DTs sufferer that he 'sees pink rats' is a further instance of this, since we don't mean here (as would be meant in a normal situation) that there are real, live pink rats which he sees . . ." (1962: 97; emphasis in text). However, to be in accordance with what Austin says about ghosts, it seems to me that he ought to say that in "*some* sense" there were these pink rats that he saw. Not of course real, live, pink rats, but hallucinatory rats.

This doesn't seem to me to be as ingrained a use of language as in the case of fictional characters. Perhaps this is because speaking of 'seeing' something here, as in 'I see a dagger,' is already rather special. There is, of course, an equally proper usage under which one would say that one doesn't see anything, one only imagines that one does. This usage is more commonly applied in this case than in the case of reference to a fictional character. 'There isn't really any dagger there; Macbeth is only having a hallucination.'

Let us now return to the original case under discussion. Here, of course, the star that is seen is real, not hallucinatory at all. But the analogy is that, as in the case of fiction we discussed before, one can have two types of predication: the out-and-out sense, and what is ascribed to it purely visually, analogously to predication according to the story. This distinction can also be applied to hallucinatory objects. 'Is hallucinatory,' 'was caused to be seen by such and such medical problems,' are out-and-out usages, whereas 'has a certain shape,' 'is colored green,' are analogous to predication "in the story."

But now I am suggesting that some of these distinctions can be applied to the star and the speck. Can such a suggestion accommodate the problems? I am not really entirely sure, but I mean to push it as far as I can in this lecture.

Why isn't the speck the star? Well, there are supposed to be plenty of arguments that the speck isn't the star. As Austin observes, if I live in my house it doesn't follow that I live in a white dot (1962: 98, note 1; quoted above). Nor could I advertise a white dot, Warnock says, though I might advertise my house. And when we continue our walk towards it, the white dot grows larger, though my house does not grow larger. And so on.

It isn't really so clear that all of this is true. Consider again the phrase 'the white dot.' Because it is a visual description of the object, it triggers the expectation that the other predicates should also be understood in this same way—according to the way the object appears. But given the right circumstances, one can properly, I think, understand them the other way. Suppose I am with a friend, and there are all sorts of dots in the horizon. I might say to him: 'Look, I live in one of the white dots; my uncle lives in one of the greenish ones.' This seems to me to be perfectly proper. Of course, one is unlikely to come out of the blue and say 'I live in a white dot': that is true. But it doesn't follow that when one has introduced 'the white dot' for this kind of description, one cannot properly go on to say, given the special circumstances, that one lives in a white dot. One could also say: 'But I am not going to live there much longer: I have advertised it in *Country Life* [that is the magazine Warnock refers to], and I think it will be snapped up.'

As we continue our walk the white dot grows larger, but my house does not grow larger. Here, of course, the predicate 'grows larger' is being applied according to the appearances. Does my house not grow larger? Well, taking this in the out-and-out sense, of course my house doesn't grow larger. But one should read this as if it were written by a novelist: 'As I zoomed in upon this house it grew larger and larger, finally looming ahead of me as a monstrous fearsome. . . .' This is perfectly all right, and in that sense, of course, my house does grow larger and larger.

What is wrong with any of that? Well, one might ask about the converse, which is a little bit harder. After all, my house stays the same size. Does the white dot in any sense stay the same size? Here, once again, the phrase 'the white dot' makes it very likely that one is going to apply predicates visually to the objects. But if one does so, then, of course, the white dot grows larger and larger. It can't stay the same size.

Look at the following very special circumstances. You say to a child, when approaching this white dot: 'See that white dot over there? It looks as if it is growing bigger and bigger, but actually that white dot is a physical object which is constant in size.' (Well, you are not likely to say to a child 'physical object which is constant in size,' so you would try and phrase it in more childish language.) You are trying to explain something about vision to the child. Under these very special circumstances, especially if you don't know which object the white dot is, so that you can't describe it in any other way, you might indeed speak of the white dot as being constant in size, though apparently growing bigger and bigger. Of course, it is very unlikely that we should say this, because once one starts with the phrase 'the white dot' one is talking about the way things look, and so one will probably apply other predicates accordingly.

Anyway, it doesn't seem to me that any case has been made for the proposition that the house isn't really identical with the white dot. It doesn't seem to me, as it does to Austin, that one should not license the conclusion that I live in a white dot.

Austin also supposes that it doesn't follow from the claimed fact that the speck is the star that we could properly say 'That very large star is a speck.' You can say that the speck is a star, but not that the large star is a speck. If that were the case, of course, the 'is' here would not be the 'is' of identity, because identity is symmetric. But *is* this the case? Suppose we have been to the star on an interplanetary ship of an appropriate sort, and now we are zooming away from the star back to the earth. Someone, maybe even without looking back, can say 'That large star is just a speck now.' Under these circumstances one *can* say that that large star is a speck. 'My house over there in the distance is that white dot, whereas Uncle Freddie's is that green dot.' These are all things that we could say.

The suggestion then would be as follows. Perhaps in the case of an original sense of 'see,' where one doesn't say of the man with a hallucination that he sees anything at all, there has to be an ordinary object out there which one sees. However, the usage gets extended by the recognition of a new and special realm of objects which are seen. At this stage one also allows a double application of predicates, either according to a visual description or out-and-out. Then if one does see an external object, predicates can be understood very naturally in either way. So, for example, when Moore sees an envelope, and says he sees something trapezoidal, the predicate is being applied visually. It doesn't follow that it isn't the envelope which he sees.

There are subtleties about all this. For one thing the whole phrase 'the way something looks' can mean various things. First, there is a way that something looks which is fairly objective, and may be different from the way it looks to me now, given some special features of the way I am looking at it. For example, the small speck in the sky may be magnified in my magnifying glass so that it appears much larger than a sixpence. So on one usage I could certainly say that, though the speck really is smaller than a sixpence, it appears larger than a sixpence because I am using a magnifying glass, or some other special kind of scope. One could also, alternatively, say 'I see a speck larger than a sixpence, because I am looking through a magnifying glass.'

So here one should really distinguish among at least three kinds of predicates: the out-and-out interpretation of the predicates ('I see a very large star'); the way the object really looks (smaller than a sixpence); and the way the object looks to me now through the magnifying glass (larger than a sixpence, but not as big as a star). These are all consistent usages, and the predicates can be applied in all of these different ways.

In the analogy with fiction here, the case is more like the one in which Napoleon appears in a story. Napoleon has out-and-out predicates that really apply to him historically, but some things are true of him only in the sense that they are ascribed to him in a story. Here the star has its out-and-out properties as an astronomical object, but also its properties (analogous to those of Napoleon in a story) as it appears to us visually.

As I say, I very much doubt if this would solve all the problems which have led people to get themselves into tangles over questions of perception, but it might apply to some of them, and I think the analogy between fiction and perception might be pushed further still, in other directions that I won't mention here.

Let me make one last remark about the example of the ghost. When someone sees a ghost, is there necessarily a ghost that he saw? The term 'ghost' here is like the term 'god,' which tends to get extended to mean 'mythical god,' perhaps because, on any view currently held (in our society, anyway, except perhaps for some very exceptional people), there are very few gods in the other sense of 'god': there are less than or equal to one, usually. So when one uses the term 'god' as a general term, it generally gets used just to mean 'mythical god.' In that sense, of course, the pagan gods really exist in the real world, because there really are such mythical entities. But in the other sense of 'god,' as meaning 'real god,' this wouldn't be true. The same would apply to the case of 'ghost.' If my cousin Josephine saw a ghost, then there is a certain hallucinatory object which she saw. If you don't "believe in ghosts" you are likely to use the term 'ghost' in just this way.

I won't, I think, continue in further elaborate detail about this kind of problem of perception, though a great deal more can be said. As I say, this kind of problem should not be mixed in with other problems about perception. When one speaks of hallucinatory objects one isn't said to be seeing one's own visual impression, or something like that. On the contrary, the visual impression of the dagger isn't a dagger, and it isn't a hallucinatory dagger, either: it isn't any kind of dagger at all. In the sense I have described, there is a hallucinatory dagger which Macbeth saw: one has an extended realm of entities.

In this kind of extended realm, which I think we are most at home with in the case of referring to fictional entities, there are two senses in which one can say that 'Hamlet exists' is true. In one sense one is reporting on what is the case inside the story: one says that it really is true, according to the story, that Hamlet exists, just as it is true that he soliloquized. The other sense is that in which there really is such a fictional character as Hamlet.

But, after all, there has got to be a sense in which there is no such person as Hamlet, in which it is correct to say that Hamlet doesn't exist. This kind of usage is that which created the original problem. And it is obviously, in some sense, prior to the usages in which one can truly say that Hamlet does exist.

I would have liked to start on the problem of this usage in this lecture, but though I have some more time I really don't have enough (only a few minutes) to start on another topic of any substance. So, having deferred this problem, which is of course the main problem people get upset about, for so long, I will discuss it next time. I feel much shakier as to what is really the truth about this kind of sentence, 'Hamlet doesn't exist,' than about any other. On my theory the problem gets more difficult, rather than easier, because understanding the term 'Hamlet' in the original way, so to speak, is merely introducing a pretense of naming. When one makes any assertion about Hamlet, one is merely pretending to express a proposition. So that should be true, it seems, of the statement that Hamlet exists, or doesn't exist, as well. And, as I said last time, one cannot ask under what circumstances Hamlet would have existed, as one would think one could if there really were a proposition being expressed when one says 'Hamlet doesn't exist.' Even worse is the fact that for me, as not for others, the problem arises also in some cases where one uses a predicate rather than making a singular existence statement. Where one says, for example, 'There are no unicorns,' what does one mean on my view? Not that though there is some definite kind of animal called a 'unicorn,' the extension of the term 'unicorn' happens to be empty. On the contrary, I deny that there is any definite kind of animal called 'the unicorn,' of which we are saying, in this kind of assertion, that the extension of the term describing it is empty.

So it is that kind of problem which I will discuss next time.[10]

10. As it turned out, this topic would not get discussed until Lecture 6, at pp. 144–59.

November 27, 1973

I am not going to do what I said I would. I decided to rearrange the order of things, because something which I was going to put at the end would be somewhat more dangling there, I now think, than it would have been if I had had two or three lectures to talk about it as I expected. But since, the way things are shaping up, I might have only one, I decided to put it in at this point.

What did I talk about in the last two lectures? Mainly I was discussing possible departures from the original paradigm, which is also the classical paradigm, for talking about such names as 'Hamlet'—that is, the paradigm according to which they have no reference, or, as I put it before, *merely pretend* to have a reference. I spoke of two uses on which these names *do* have reference. One was the "in the story" kind of use, where we should say, speaking as a report on what is said in the story, that the name 'Hamlet' really refers to a person, though 'Gonzago' does not. And second, when the ontology of fictional characters is recognized, we then say that the name 'Hamlet' really refers to a fictional character; the name 'Zeus' refers to a real mythical figure or legendary god. Whereas the name 'Moloch,' if the theories that I was describing previously are right, does not refer to any such entity—it was only thought to refer to a mythical god, or to a legendary god. In any case, where such names as 'Zeus' and 'Hamlet' would, on the original paradigm, have been empty, they would have a reference on this new paradigm. So these are two uses on which the name 'Hamlet' can have a reference.

I also went on to say that using this ontology of fictional characters can enable us to see what is meant by various statements in ordinary language where we seem to relate to a fictional object; and perhaps this even extends to the case of perception, and our relations to perceptual objects. More important for the case of perception was the observation that fictional characters, when predicates are applied to them, can be described in two ways. First, there is the "out-and-out" way, according to their true properties as fictional characters—being invented, say, by such-and-such an author at such-and-such a time. Second, the predicates can be applied fictionally according to what is said—what is attached to that name—in the story, as when we say that Frankenstein's monster was created in a certain year which is not the year that that *fictional character* was in fact created. I suggested that the same thing might apply to various perceptual cases where we apply incompatible predicates in two different descriptions of a perceptual object;[1] and that rather than positing two different perceptual objects here, we can instead posit that just these two different forms of language are being used.

In any event, we have here two ways in which such an empty name as 'Hamlet' can have reference. Now, there is a third way which is mentioned in the literature, and which I haven't discussed. So let me do so. It is mostly introduced in the literature in connection not with proper names but with definite descriptions. Donnellan's article on definite descriptions especially has made this case famous (see Donnellan 1966). There is a previous article by Leonard Linsky (Linsky 1963), and there are other anticipations in the literature as well.[2]

---

1. Though in this case, the better analogy is not to two incompatible descriptions of a fictional character but, rather, of a historical person who may also be described incompatibly in a fictional work, like Napoleon, the example mentioned in the previous lectures.

2. As I said before (Lecture I, note 4), the discussion in the remainder of this lecture is developed further in Kripke (1977). For other anticipations, see note 19 below.

The case given by Linsky and developed by Donnellan is this one. Suppose someone says of an unmarried woman, 'Her husband is kind to her.' Then on Russell's view what he has said must be false. On the paradigm of Frege (1892) and[3] Strawson (1950) what he has said is neither true nor false, or "lacking in truth value." In both cases there is an implication or presupposition that the description is fulfilled, in this case, that she has a husband. As Donnellan says:

> Both Russell and Strawson assume that where the presupposition or implication is false, the truth value of what the speaker says is affected. For Russell the statement made is false; for Strawson it has no truth value.

> (1966: 283)

Donnellan's basic challenge to Russell and Strawson is this: need we accept either one of these? Need we accept that it is false, or that it is neither true nor false? After all, when someone says 'her husband,' there may be a man that he saw whom he *took to be* her husband. He observed that that man was kind to her. Surely then he is referring when he uses the phrase 'her husband': he is referring to the man he was talking about. What he said of that man is true if the man in question is in fact kind to her. So, on the classical Russellian paradigm, and also on Frege's and Strawson's view, the relevant utterance of the phrase 'her husband' would have no referent.[4] But perhaps one should say, on the contrary, that it obviously *does* have a referent, for even though the woman is not married, the phrase

---

3. Actually, Donnellan never refers to Frege. After Strawson's paper for a while the dispute became well-known as one between Russell and Strawson, and Frege's views were forgotten or ignored, even though Frege is explicitly criticized in Russell's paper.

4. Actually, of course, in Russell's theory, definite descriptions are not referring expressions at all. But he would say that they have no denotation, where the denotation of a definite description is the unique object filling the description. I ignore such distinctions most of the time.

'her husband' refers here to the man the speaker was talking about. And it is this view which I wish to discuss today. Of course, if it was true, it would give another sense in which an "empty" designator, here a definite description, could have a referent.

Donnellan, on the basis of this kind of example, introduces a distinction between referential and attributive uses of definite descriptions. The attributive use can be roughly characterized as the use where one is willing to add a phrase of the kind 'whoever she (he, it) is.' This may not be a strict characterization but it will give flavor.[5] As an example (given by Donnellan), we see a man in the dock in a murder trial, and say 'Smith's murderer is insane.' What do we mean? Well, according to Donnellan we might mean two things, depending on the context and our motivation.

Suppose the murder is so grisly that we think that whoever did it was insane. Then we mean to say of the murderer, whoever he is, that he is insane. We would say that was so, whether or not the man in the dock really is the murderer, whether or not we believe the man in the dock to be the murderer. We may believe the man in the dock to be the murderer, but at any rate we are saying of the murderer, whoever he is, that he is insane. And we could even put in the phrase here 'whoever he is': 'Smith's murderer, whoever he is, is insane' (or 'must be insane').

On the other hand, we may notice the behavior of the defendant in the dock, and, taking him to be Smith's murderer, refer to him and say of him that he is insane. In this usage we could put in a

---

5. Searle (1979) in fact noted that in one of Donnellan's referential examples one could add 'whoever he is . . .'; 'The man over there drinking a martini, whoever he is, is a spy (or whatever).' Moreover, of course, in an attributive case, 'whoever he is' might be a bizarre thing to add when the speaker feels completely sure who fits the description. The real point is that the speaker intends to be talking about the thing fitting the description, and his intentions are exhausted by that characterization. Donnellan's idea is expounded in the paragraphs directly following.

parenthetical clause, '(that is, that man)': 'Smith's murderer (that is, that man) is insane.' (It would be, of course, more natural in fact to reverse the clauses: 'That man—that is, Smith's murderer—is insane.') Here we are saying just of a particular person that he is insane, and what we say is true of him even if, in fact, he is innocent: even if there was no murderer, we can say that we truly spoke of him, and said of him that he was insane. This would be the case if, say, Smith had actually committed suicide, and the man was being quite unjustly accused. The Frege-Strawson account would give this phrase 'Smith's murderer' an empty reference, but perhaps we should say that it is not the case that there is no reference: rather, we were talking about the man in the dock. This is the referential use of a definite description.

Notice that in the attributive use, if there is no murderer, then there really is no reference. If we were saying 'Smith's murderer, whoever he is, must be insane,' and in fact Smith was in such a state that he committed suicide in a grisly and insane way, in that case the traditional conditions are not satisfied, and the phrase 'Smith's murderer' has no reference.[6]

A very good example in support of Donnellan's picture might be the case of a hypothetical religious work, similar perhaps to the Gospels,[7] which normally (or even always) refers to its hero as 'the Messiah.' If we are asking whether this work is a true or false account of the person it is talking about, we don't ask whether he really is the

---

6. I suppose that this kind of account could be applied to a putative empty name too, though it has a less plausible ring to me in that case. You meet someone and wrongly take him to be, say, Hamlet. But still, there *was* a person whom you were talking about, and perhaps one should say, following Donnellan, that the name 'Hamlet' really did have a referent in such a context.

7. In Kripke (1977; 2011a: 101) I say that this example was suggested by a remark of L. Crocker. There may be, of course, other examples than the Gospels, e.g., a follower of Shabbetai Zvi might write such an account of his life.

Messiah, or even, if there is one, whether the person so characterized in the work really fits the bill. Suppose there isn't one: that would not in and of itself make us inclined—so it might be argued—to declare the entire work historically false from beginning to end, provided it truly predicates of the person the writer referred to as 'the Messiah' various appropriate properties, activities, and so on.

Donnellan says that though Russell's theory, and Strawson's also, as he describes it, may give a correct account of the attributive use, it doesn't give a correct account of the referential use. These are two different uses, and Russell at most gives a correct account of one. Strawson, he appears to think, intends to give an account of definite descriptions as referential, but often fails since he does not recognize what Donnellan thinks of as the essential feature of the referential use. In any case Russell's account, he thinks, would uniformly, if correct, apply to the attributive case but would fail as an analysis of the referential use.

I want to examine this view and see if it creates another exception here. Of course, though Donnellan generally emphasizes cases where Russell would say that the phrase has no denotation—for example, in the case where the woman in question has no husband, isn't married—his arguments apply just as well to the case where there *is* some unique thing fitting the description, though it is not the thing that the speaker was discussing. So, instead of concentrating on the case where one says of an unmarried woman, 'Her husband is kind to her,' one can say this of a married woman one saw with a man, being under the misconception that that man is her husband.[8] If so, we are still talking about that man, the man taken here to be her husband. There are other, subtler cases given by Donnellan,

---

8. In fact, the man may be her lover to whom she was driven precisely because of the cruelty of her husband!

where no one is under a misconception, but still another entity is being referred to: for example, the use of 'the king' by a group all of whom regard the man they are talking about as an illegitimate usurper, and not the real king, but who nevertheless, out of prudence, adopt this phrase, using it to refer to the usurper. It is common knowledge among the participants that the use is hypocritical.

To me it is a little hard to examine Donnellan's views exactly, because they don't seem to be clearly consistent, and depending on which of the strains in his line one may emphasize, I might agree or disagree. He first says that he has refuted Russell, or shown the inadequacy of Russell's theory as a general account of the matter. Second, he says that though he has noticed an ambiguity between the referential and the attributive use, it should not be regarded as a semantic ambiguity, nor as a syntactic ambiguity. In fact, he doesn't think it is an ambiguity in the sentence at all. Instead it is some kind of "pragmatic ambiguity": the distinction between the roles a description plays is a function of the speaker's intentions.

Since such phrases as 'semantic ambiguity,' 'pragmatic ambiguity,' 'syntactic ambiguity,' and so on have partly to me the air of slogans until they are fleshed out, it is not utterly clear to me what he means. But it would seem to me that, if he is right that there is no semantic ambiguity, then there is only one analysis of a sentence containing a definite description. If there were two, that would be what I would call a "semantic ambiguity."

Take such an expression as 'The cops are coming.' This has only, I suppose, one analysis—or let's suppose that it does (maybe the term 'cops' can mean more than one thing). But it can be used in various ways. It can be used as a warning, or as an expression of relief, or for various other purposes. These are pragmatic ambiguities. One criminal may say to another—a burglar, say, in the midst of the burglary: 'The cops are coming.' He need not be taken to be in a strong sense asserting that the cops are coming. Of course he *is* asserting this, but he may say this even though his hearer knows that the cops are coming, that his hearer knows that he, the speaker, knows that the cops are coming, and so on. In fact, both of them know that the other knows that the cops are coming. This has a couple of technical names in various kinds of literature. Everyone may know that everyone else knows that the cops are coming, but the burglar is saying this to convey 'Look, we can't waste our time getting this stuff; we'd better quit here because the cops are coming.'

This might be a very special use of the sentence, 'The cops are coming.' It doesn't fit into the kind of paradigm that one might get from Grice's article on meaning (Grice 1957). That is, the speaker is not intending to induce a belief that the cops are coming; he is not intending to induce a belief that he believes that the cops are coming—or any iteration of this. I don't know whether this is a counterexample to something that Grice says because there have been so many redefinitions that I have really lost my grip: I would have to do a little more checking or figuring out. At any rate, it is certainly a counterexample to a crude Gricean paradigm. But though it is a special usage, and though one can say that when the burglar said 'The cops are coming' he meant *don't waste time trying to grab any more gems: let's get the hell out of here*, nevertheless this doesn't give a case for an alternative analysis, in this instance, of the phrase 'The cops are coming.' It has a uniform semantic analysis, though here, as a matter of some kind of pragmatics, it is being used in a fairly special way.

Suppose Donnellan meant that the uses of definite descriptions were only pragmatically, but not semantically, ambiguous, in the way that this was clearly true of the burglar's remark. Then it would be impossible to say that Russell has given a correct analysis of the attributive use but not of the referential use, because one doesn't give an analysis *of a use* in this sense at all. One gives different readings for an ambiguous sentence, if it is ambiguous. If it isn't ambiguous it has only one reading, and Russell would be either uniformly correct or uniformly incorrect. One can't maintain that he is correct for some cases and not correct for others, and at the same time that the sentence is not semantically ambiguous. One can maintain that a sentence with a given uniform reading could be used in very special ways in special contexts because of various special principles of conversation, but not that it is both unambiguous and has two different readings. Perhaps Donnellan means something here that I haven't grasped, but I want just to set this aside, and ask a question which is clearer than are such phrases as 'semantic ambiguity' and 'pragmatic ambiguity': is the argument given by Donnellan an argument against Russell's analysis of definite descriptions? I don't mean here to maintain that Russell's analysis is correct: I am just setting it up as, so to speak, a paradigm to compare Donnellan's remarks with, as sort of a methodological device in discussing the merits of this kind of criticism of Russell. It may be that there is some other argument against Russell that would be correct, even if Donnellan's methodology did not give a correct argument against him.

What should be said about this? First, if Donnellan took the strong line that the speaker's statement that her husband is kind to her is true (whether or not she has a husband, or if she has one, whether or not he is kind to her), and if the speaker were correct in so saying, then of course we would have a refutation of Russell. We would also have, I think, a very obvious argument that the statement is semantically ambiguous, because its truth conditions would be different from the truth conditions given by Russell. And if the truth conditions supplied by Russell would apply in some cases, and some other set of truth conditions in another case, then that is as strong a case for semantic ambiguity as I can imagine to hold. But Donnellan doesn't quite, in fact, come down and say that even when the man the speaker is talking about isn't her husband, so long as he is kind to her, it doesn't matter whether her real husband is kind to her; so long as *this* man is kind to her the sentence expresses a truth. He doesn't say this because, of course, this leads to the somewhat awkward result that when the speaker said that her husband was kind to her, he said truly that her husband was kind to her, whereas in fact her husband isn't kind to her. Even if we know the facts, we would have to say this on the assumption in question.

Donnellan doesn't want to get such a result, so he says, more delicately, that we can't say what statement was made: it can't really quite be reported in our language because we cannot use the phrase 'her husband' referentially to refer to that man. Instead we can say that he truly said *of* the man he was referring to that he is kind to her. And the same delicate remarks would apply in his other cases. (See section VIII of Donnellan 1966.)

Since these remarks are delicate they aren't out-and-out incompatible with Russell. To investigate the question of to what degree these remarks of Donnellan's may in fact constitute a refutation of Russell, and make us recognize another dimension of reference, I will introduce some methodological distinctions. First, we have to distinguish, just as in the case of 'The cops are coming,' between what we might say that the speaker meant by his words (which, in that very crude and obvious case, was *let's get out of here!*—he wasn't informing someone that the cops were coming) and what *the words* mean, even when said by a particular speaker on a special occasion (that is, in this case as in any other, *that the police are coming*).

Second, I wish to emphasize a methodological principle which comes (though I have given it a somewhat different form) from

Grice (1975).[9] Grice, as you know, emphasizes in his work the differ-ence between (a) putting various implications of what the speaker says into a theory of the conventional meaning of his words, a theory of what his words mean, and (b) applying various general principles of language which would allow us to deduce from the speaker's words, with a given fixed and weaker meaning, the other implica-tions that are drawn. An example of this would be the case of conjunction—of 'and.' Various people have argued that in English as opposed to logic the word 'and' either is ambiguous between a mere conjunction and something indicating temporal sequence, or it actually uniformly implies as part of its meaning some kind of temporal sequence, so that when you say 'I got up in the morning and brushed my teeth' you imply not only that you did both, but that you got up in the morning first. (Of course in this case one might infer this ordering for other reasons: it is unlikely that you would have brushed your teeth before you got up in the morning. But another example to the same point could be given.) Grice, on the contrary, wishes to test such views that these things are part of the meaning of 'and' against an alternative hypothesis that the meaning of 'and' is merely a matter of conjunction (in the normal truth-functional sense in logic), though it is a general principle about languages that (at least in this sort of case) a speaker is likely to narrate events in the order in which they happen. And so, rather than being part of the meaning of the word 'and,' the tendency to infer that you brushed your teeth second comes simply from the application of this general principle.[10]

---

9. I heard these matters discussed by Grice in seminars and perhaps even these lectures them-selves, before they got into print.
10. I now (2012) have my doubts about this particular example (that the ordinary use of 'and' does not ever conventionally imply temporal sequence, and the Gricean argument stan-dardly given for it). But the general methodological point remains.

This type of methodology I want to apply here in a special way. The following, I think, should be a test of any view that a particular kind of example is a refutation of a particular kind of semantical theory. Suppose we say that an example of kind E or linguistic behavior of kind E shows that a certain kind of semantical theory, or a certain analysis of English sentences, is wrong. A test of this kind of argument would be to imagine a hypothetical community, perhaps not our own, in which the analysis given by the semantical theory in question is stipulated to be correct; if it isn't a correct analysis of English, then they are not speaking English. (Of course, one has to be sure that the semantical theory is coherent, in the sense that there could be a language which has this kind of analysis. But in many cases we can be clear enough about that.) One then tests whether there are some general conversational maxims, which might apply to all languages, that show that in the case of this stipulated hypothetical language the linguistic features which were supposed to yield the counterexample—linguistic features of kind E—are actually exhibited. If they are, then the example can be no counterexample to the thesis that the semantical theory in question gives the correct analysis of English, because a hypothetical language which stipulatively satisfied this analysis would exhibit these same features.

Let me give a brief example of this. I won't perhaps go into it at enough length really to establish it. Some people have argued that identity must be a relation between names, that is, a metalinguistic relation rather than a relation between an object and itself. 'What is the point of having a relation between an object and itself?' 'What are you saying about the objects?' And so on. We can test whether this is a good argument in favor of the metalinguistic theory, as against the theory that identity is a relation which holds only between an object and itself, by imagining a hypothetical language in which a relation, call it 'schmidentity,' was stipulatively introduced as relating only each object and itself. Some might argue that such a stipulation is incoherent. I don't see that it is. Why can't we have a relation with that stipulated extension? At any rate, all the philosophical problems about Hesperus and Phosphorus which are supposed to be conclusive against identity as a relation between an object and itself would arise in this hypothetical language for the problem of *schmidentity*. Therefore they cannot be arguments that ordinary identity is not such a relation, for the features that were supposed to give rise to problems would arise in this hypothetical language also. And I think we could say this even without knowing what the solutions are to all the philosophical problems about identity statements. We can say in advance that this is no argument that identity is not a relation between a thing and itself.[11]

I want to apply this to the case of a hypothetical language in which Russell's theory was introduced by stipulation as the correct theory. So the stipulation that we make (it is supposed to be set up by the analogue of the *Académie Française*) is that 'The ϕ ψs' is to mean 'There is something which uniquely ϕs, and it ψs,' in notation which I think I have already introduced in these lectures:

$$1.\ (\exists x)(\varphi!x \wedge \psi x)$$

(Again, $\phi!x$ in my notation means: x is the unique thing satisfying ϕ.)[12] An argument, if it is an argument against Russell's theory, would show that this hypothetical language would diverge from English in some specifiable way. I don't want to examine the general question of whether this language would diverge from English, but just whether in the type of case mentioned by Donnellan we would have a divergence from English. We can call it "the Russell language."

11. This parallels the discussion in *N&N* (1972/1980: 108).
12. See Lecture II, note 3.

One can even refer to another hypothetical language, which I could call "the ultra-Russell language," in which definite descriptions beginning with the word 'the' aren't used at all. Instead one always replaces them by their Russellian expansions. So instead of saying 'The ϕ ψs,' you always have to say 'something ϕs, and uniquely, and it ψs.' This would be an even more Russellian language because even the abbreviation 'the' wouldn't be allowed to be introduced.

One of the kinds of cases Donnellan has in mind is this. One says of a man in some corner of the room at a party, 'The man over there drinking champagne looks happy.'[13] What you have said is true of him, Donnellan says, even if he isn't drinking champagne—actually he is a teetotaler who just has water in his glass, but this has little relevance to your reference. Even if there is no one in the room drinking champagne, or if there is a unique person, other than that man, drinking champagne in the room, what you say is about *him*, the man you have in mind: the definite description is being used as if it were just a name, as if it were a mere tag, and you have said something truly or falsely of *him*. (The question whether the statement is true or false is hedged: you say something truly or falsely of him, depending on whether he is happy or not.)

What would go on in the Russell language? First, if someone is over in the corner and you think he is drinking champagne, certainly you could just as well in the Russell language say 'The man over there in the corner drinking champagne is happy,' because the fact that you are a speaker of the Russell language doesn't guarantee you any infallibility, of course, about who is the unique person fitting the

---

13. Both in the original version of this lecture and in Kripke (1977) I switched Donnellan's original example from 'a martini' to 'champagne.' This was sheer inadvertence on my part. I don't know whether it makes any difference, but I have kept my original mistake here.

Donnellan also gives an example of the 'attributive' use of the martini (or champagne) case.

description. And if you think it is that man, and you don't know his name, and you think it is impolite to point, or to say 'that man,' you may well use the phrase 'the man over there drinking champagne' and think that you have been talking about him when you say 'The man over there drinking champagne is happy.' So this is certainly not a case of divergent behavior.

In the ultra-Russell language, of course, you would have to use a circumlocution. But if you don't know the man's name, and you don't have definite descriptions in the language, and you want to talk about him without pointing or saying 'that man,' you may very well say, in order to identify him, 'Someone over there in the corner is drinking champagne and is happy.' In English, of course, this would be more natural under special circumstances: there is what might be called an 'arch' use of the phrase 'someone,' or 'a certain someone' (or even, in philosophical circles, 'there exists an x'), as in 'There is a certain someone over in the corner of the room drinking champagne and he is having an affair with Smith's wife.' This would be a natural-sounding usage even in English as we have it today. If one didn't have definite descriptions such usages might become more widespread, even in more commonplace cases.

So far, then, we have come across nothing that shows that we do not speak the Russell language. Perhaps something about the other features of the situation shows this? For example, we can say that he said something true (false) about the man he was talking about. Can we say this in the Russell language?

Let me first mention another case. You see a man in the distance and you take him to be Smith: in fact you have mistaken him—it is Jones. 'What is Smith doing?' someone asks, and I reply 'He is raking the leaves.' It is clear who is being talked about, namely the man over there who in fact has been mistaken for Smith—it is Jones. Should we then say that this case provides a counterexample to various theories of proper names? Should we say that it shows that a proper name 'Smith' must be multiply ambiguous, even if there were only one person in the world actually called 'Smith'? Should we say that here 'Smith' is being used as a name of Jones?

It seems to me to be plain that that is not the case. Here, as elsewhere, the speakers (speaking their own language) were using 'Smith' as a name of Smith, and not of Jones; but since they mistook Smith for James in this instance they were in some sense referring to Jones. They were *talking about* Jones. So one should distinguish between what I might call the "speaker's reference," which answers to such queries as 'Who was the speaker talking about when he used such and such proper name?' The answer to the question 'What is the referent of this name in the speaker's language?' I might call the "semantic reference" of the name in his language. When the speaker said 'Smith is raking the leaves' he was talking about Jones: the speaker's reference was Jones. But does that mean that the name 'Smith' is in his idiolect sometimes the name of Smith and under certain special circumstances a name of Jones? Of course not: the name 'Smith' is just a name of Smith—that is what I call the "semantic reference," the thing that the name is a name of. The speaker was able to talk about Jones by using the name 'Smith,' in this instance, because both he and his hearer mistook Jones for Smith. They weren't really very concerned that they should be talking about Smith: they were only concerned to talk about that man in the distance, and they would have amended their remarks if they had known the true facts.[14]

---

14. It could be mentioned that Church (1995: 69) seems to think that it is *only* speakers who refer, presumably even without using any explicit term designating the object, and that the use of 'reference' and 'referent' in philosophical literature is a repugnant violation of normal English usage. Maybe so, but probably under the influence of Max Black's translation of Frege (1892; 1997e), the usage has become too standard in philosophy to give up.

This, then, is why they were able to use the name in this way. There is no argument here that the proper name 'Smith' is ambiguous, even in this speaker's idiolect. Of course, other such cases could arise which are subtler, like Donnellan's special usurper case. Suppose there were someone, an impostor, who in order to gain an inheritance had been passing himself off as Smith; and everyone doesn't want to offend this impostor, though they know that he is a fraud—for some special reason they don't want to offend him. They might then refer to him as 'Smith,' knowing that he isn't Smith. This kind of case is a little more special—both Donnellan's usurper case and this one I have just described—because now you are making statements that you know to be literally false, though you still say something true perhaps about the person you are referring to.

In this case, too, there is no basis for arguing that the name is ambiguous: the example shows, rather, that the speaker's reference on this occasion diverges from the semantic reference. A semantic reference in a speaker's idiolect gives his general intentions. He forms a general intention such as: 'When I use the name "Smith" I shall refer to that man.' (Who "that man" is has to be specified.) In a specific instance he may think that he is fulfilling this intention, even when he isn't. His primary intention in the specific instance may be to talk about that man over there raking leaves; and since he thinks that that man over there raking the leaves is Smith, he thinks that he has fulfilled his general intention when he utters 'Smith is raking the leaves.' But though he thinks his specific intentions on this occasion are a fulfillment of his general intentions, in fact they are not. This is the simplest and the most standard way in which speaker's reference and semantic reference diverge.

This is obviously a general principle about language which would be exemplified in any kind of language which has referring expressions. One may always distinguish between what you are talking about, and what the semantic referent is of the term you use. These need not be the same. Sometimes it will be ambiguous what you are talking about, as between an intended referent and a semantic referent, as it might be in the leaf-raking case if one asks, 'Who were the speakers talking about?' Depending on how interested they were in the (supposed) fact that it was *Smith* who was raking the leaves, they could be said to be talking either about Smith and not the man raking the leaves, or about the man raking leaves and not Smith, or, once the true facts are known, ambiguously about both. But the semantic referent is unambiguously Smith.

There seems to be no reason why this kind of methodology cannot be applied also in the case of a definite description. Suppose one uses a definite description 'the ϕ.' Then one has a general intention to refer, when one uses 'the ϕ,' to *the* thing which uniquely satisfies ϕ.[15] If one comes across something which one thinks uniquely satisfies ϕ, one will think one is fulfilling this intention by using the description 'the ϕ' to talk about it. And it may be that your primary interest is to talk about "it" irrespective of its satisfying ϕ: all the same, you do think that you are in accord with your general semantic intention here. But you may not be, for something else may be 'the ϕ.'

Here one may very well be talking unambiguously about, say, *that thing over there*, thinking that it uniquely satisfies ϕ, when in fact

---

15. Here, of course, one's general intention to use a description to refer to the thing that uniquely satisfies ϕ follows from the general semantical rules for the definite article and those for the understanding of predicates. I wouldn't have to add this obvious fact, except that at least one critic of my previously published paper on this topic (Kripke 1977) professed to take me as denying this and assuming that speakers form each such intention separately. Not only is this obviously not the case, the hypothetical Russell language that I postulate plainly would give a general rule for the semantics of the descriptions.

Clearly, general intentions can follow from more general ones. For example, someone may not keep his liquor store open on Sundays, as a general policy. But this may be because he has a more general policy of obeying the law of his own jurisdiction, which includes this. The semantic case is far more complicated, but the point is illustrated by this simple one.

either nothing uniquely satisfies ϕ, or something else does. In that case you weren't in any sense at all, perhaps, talking about the *other thing* which does in fact satisfy ϕ: your whole intention was to talk about *that thing over there*, just as, perhaps, your whole intention may have been to talk about *that man raking the leaves*. In the case of a definite description, though, it is even more likely that there should be no ambiguity about who you were talking about—about what the speaker's reference was—because one is talking about a thing over there, and uses 'the ϕ' simply to characterize it. One isn't using 'the ϕ' as a name of an object which is in fact called something else: one is using 'the ϕ' to characterize an object. If the object isn't characterized by 'the ϕ' you don't in this case care what other object may be characterized by 'the ϕ.' In the case of Smith and Jones it would be proper to say, even if they were solely interested in talking about Jones, that they confused him with Smith. But it would not be the case with the man supposedly drinking champagne that they confused him with some other man actually drinking champagne, even if there is another person uniquely drinking champagne in that area of the room. Rather, they simply erroneously thought that that man could be characterized—described—as drinking champagne. That is why descriptions are called 'descriptions' rather than 'names'—because they describe.

Does this distinction between speaker's reference and semantic reference apply to the hypothetical Russell language? It seems to me that there is no reason why it shouldn't. We can say that the speaker's reference (in the case of the simple kind of Russell language imagined) is the thing which they *thought* satisfied the definite description, and which they wanted to talk about. They talked about it by using the definite description they did, because they thought it uniquely satisfied it. Even if they used the unabbreviated forms, because they were forced to—because definite descriptions weren't to be found in the language—they might talk about "that thing over there" by saying: 'there is an *x* which *φ*s'—which may be *drinking champagne*—'and which has some other property *ψ*'—say, *being happy*. In none of these cases is there any reason to say that the analysis of the definite description in the Russell language is not precisely as given. It was stipulated that that was to be the analysis. The distinctions could be drawn even if we didn't use the definite description itself but used the unabbreviated form, 'there is some-one over there. . . .' Suppose you said in ordinary English, where in the "arch" use such a circumlocution would be natural, 'Someone over there is drinking champagne, and he is having an affair with Mrs. Smith.' Then there was a person whom you gossiped about as having an affair with Mrs. Smith, even if he wasn't drinking cham-pagne. Even if some other unique person in the room was drinking champagne, you weren't gossiping about *him*—you were gossiping about the other man. So it makes no difference if the long circumlo-cutionary form is explicitly used.

The usurper-type cases have to be explained in another way, but I will leave this as an exercise for the hearer (or reader). They don't seem to me to represent any special difficulty. They are a special and a funny kind of case, as Donnellan himself mentions. (The explana-tion would be in terms of the thing that was being officially regarded as satisfying the predicates—as the value that cashes them in—rather than in terms of the thing the speaker and hearer believe to cash them in.)

So it would seem that, as applied to a hypothetical Russellian language, even the ultra-Russellian language where actual definite descriptions are replaced by their analyses, all the distinctions in question could be drawn. These should not be taken as distinctions between two different senses of a definite description. Rather, what we have are special cases of a general principle about reference, namely that a distinction has to be made between the semantic reference of a name or of a singular term, which corresponds to the general intentions the speaker forms of how he will use that name or term, and the speaker's reference in using that name or term on a particular occasion, which corresponds to the speaker's specific intentions on a particular occasion, intentions which he may think fulfill his general intentions even if they do not.

This, I want to suggest, is the true explanation of the phenomenon pointed out by Donnellan. If so, Donnellan has given no argument against Russell. The reason why it seems to me to be clear that there isn't an argument against Russell here is, as I said, that Donnellan's remarks would apply to a hypothetical language in which an *Académie Française* stipulatively set up Russell's truth conditions as the actual truth conditions and set up Russell's analysis as the correct analysis. If Donnellan had argued (and successfully), in the case of 'Her husband is kind to her,' that the statement itself really has different truth conditions from the ones Russell would say it has, then of course if he were right we would have a phenomenon which would prove that our language is not the Russell language. But it seems to me to be right on Donnellan's part not to say definitely that the truth conditions of the statement are different. Do we really want to say that the statement 'Her husband is kind to her,' said on a particular occasion, was true, when in fact her husband is the cruelest man on earth to his wife, and we would say so? Shouldn't we instead say that when the speaker said 'Her husband is kind to her' he said something true about the man he was talking about? Or even, perhaps, that when he said this, *what he meant* was true—though that is not the same thing as the analysis of the statement 'Her husband is kind to her'? As I said, Donnellan *is* cautious about this: he doesn't go against what I have said, and I think rightly. If so, a feature of language has not been pointed out which would contradict Russell's theory.

This can clear up various things that people have said about proper names. I have heard argued against me (not just recently, but before), in the case given in *N&N* where Gödel was an impostor who wrongly took over the work of a man named Schmidt, that surely in some special circumstances the name 'Gödel' is being used as a name for 'the man who *really* proved the incompleteness of arithmetic' (Kripke 1972/80: 83–84). I used this example to show that 'Gödel' doesn't mean 'the man who proved the incompleteness of arithmetic,' and that its reference isn't so determined. But some have said: 'Look, at least in some circumstances this is so. When a group of people are talking just about Gödel's theorem, surely they are using the name 'Gödel' just to refer to whoever did this work. And if Gödel was a fraud who took over someone else's work, that doesn't matter. At least in this kind of case, they are using the name 'Gödel' as a name for whoever really did the work, which in this case would be Schmidt.

Well, I would be inclined to suppose that if under certain circumstances this is so, and the people were using 'Gödel' in that manner, this is another case of speaker's reference. The speaker who thought someone was drinking champagne would withdraw his characterization of the subject if he were apprised of the facts, as would the speaker who says something about Jones but mistakenly thinks it is Smith. Similarly, if they say something such as 'Oh, how marvelous was Gödel's diagonalization device!,' they would withdraw the use of 'Gödel' and replace it by 'Schmidt' if they learned that it was the latter who had actually invented the device.

Now, let us return to the issue between Russell and Donnellan. What shall we say about the case of definite descriptions? All I have really said is that Donnellan hasn't given an argument against Russell. This doesn't of course show that the language doesn't conform to a Donnellan-type pattern as opposed to a Russellian one.

Donnellan himself might be regarded (though because of his hedges it is unclear whether he should be so regarded) as setting up a hypothetical alternative language of his own which we could also compare to English. In this language 'the ϕ' is ambiguous—let's say semantically ambiguous, no matter what he says in the paper. On one reading 'The ϕ ψs' is to be analyzed according to Russell. On the other reading 'the ϕ' is to refer to a certain man or thing—say, the thing the speaker believes to satisfy ϕ (that would be the simplest case); and the statement is analyzed so that it is true if and only if the thing he believes to satisfy ϕ also satisfies ψ.[16]

This is a hypothetical language, and of course it too would exhibit the features Donnellan points out, because Donnellan's hypothesis was tailored to explain these features. So we haven't adjudicated between the two cases, except in as much as we may apply a maxim which says that we are not to postulate ambiguities where they are not needed—that we should adopt a uniform account, plus general linguistic principles, rather than an account which gives two separate meanings whose relations then have to be explained.

Let me say a little bit more in favor of this kind of principle of parsimony as it applies in this case. Consider a language, say Swahili, which contains definite descriptions—possibly it doesn't; but suppose it does—and assume that in this language they use definite descriptions only attributively. If they use, say, 'the' for attributive descriptions, one could imagine that they use, say, 'ze' for referential descriptions. If it were true that a definite description in English had two apparently unrelated meanings in the same way that *bank* and *bank* are two meanings of the word 'bank'—I suppose you know what

---

16. In the last section of his paper, Donnellan compares the referential use of definite descriptions to Russell's notion of genuine proper names (logically proper names). If we ignore Russell's view that only a small number of special objects can be named in this way, this might be an appropriate way of looking at this hypothetical language.

I mean!—then one would expect, I think, *a priori* that one would not hear a report that descriptions exhibit the same ambiguity in Swahili.[17]

And if my own expectations were right, and the opposite was reported—that descriptions in Swahili do exhibit a parallel ambiguity—then some unifying principle has to be found, for the latter report would appear to contradict the supposition that the two uses are really unrelated. The unifying principle should apply both to English and to our hypothetical Swahili. I think the natural unifying principle here is very plausibly just that of speaker's reference. For how does this kind of case arise? It arises because one can think that a certain man over there is drinking champagne—or that a certain man is this woman's husband—even when he isn't. And one then uses an inappropriate description to talk about him. This is exactly like the case with proper names which I will take to be undisputed—'Smith over there is raking the leaves.'[18]

This provides a natural unifying principle which would lead us to expect that in our hypothetical Swahili we would inevitably have the same linguistic phenomena. I have proposed one unitary account. Someone who disagrees with me, or thinks that I am wrong, might either propose an alternative unitary account (which might agree with Russell's theory—or it might not), or she might propose an account which shows how, where there are two senses, one of them is naturally parasitic on, or arises out of, the other. But it is up to her to provide an account.

The account that I have provided seems to me to be *the* natural one for this kind of case. And it favors the unitary view that Russell's

---

17. I can't really be expounding Donnellan's actual view here. We have seen already that he doesn't postulate a real semantic ambiguity. All the more so, he cannot really be imagining two *unrelated* meanings like *bank* and *bank*.
18. Of course there are languages with no definite article (and/or with no indefinite article). These cases are not relevant.

analysis, if correct at all, is uniformly correct. I am not saying here that Russell's analysis really is correct—I am not taking a stand on this; I am just using Russell's view as a very clean and appropriate example of a unitary analysis—but that *some* unitary analysis should be given, and that the cases noted by Donnellan should just be explained by the general principle of the divergence of speaker's reference from semantic reference.

But so far what I have said doesn't provide any phenomenon that would adjudicate, in terms of actual linguistic behavior, between an ambiguity view—or a Donnellan-type view, to the extent it can be so regarded—and a unitary view. It would be much nicer if the difference between these two hypothetical languages, if they really are two different hypothetical languages, would actually show up in the speaker's linguistic behavior. In fact I found a little sub-phenomenon, in English anyway, which I thought might be used to adjudicate between the two rival views. Geach actually mentions very briefly the notion of speaker's reference, the notion of reference as applied to a particular person: he actually even gives a Donnellan kind of example (Geach 1962: 8).[19] And he says that this is of negligible importance for logic. I myself say in a footnote to *N&N* (1972/80: 25, note 3), just very briefly discussing what I have been discussing here at length, that the whole batch of phenomena pointed out by Donnellan is of very little importance for semantics, though it may be important for a theory of speech acts. I don't any longer think that this is completely true. I think it has the following kind of importance for the semantics of pronominalization.

19. Thanks to Neale (1990: 112, note 37), I am also now aware of Hampshire (1959: 201–4), which anticipates a great deal of the subsequent discussion of Donnellan's type of example of referential use.

I think someone once told me that such examples appeared in Oxford philosophy exams (long before Donnellan's paper was published), and the question was raised whether they constitute a problem for Russell's theory of descriptions. Moreover, both Neale and Oster-tag (1998: 32, note 29) mention an early anticipation by the Port-Royal grammarians.

Consider the following two dialogues, both of them boring. A couple of you have heard them before.

> *Dialogue No. 1*: (This occurs in the case where someone sees a married woman with a man and takes him for her husband, who is actually someone else.) *A* says 'Her husband is kind to her.' *B* is someone who knows the facts. So then *B* may say 'He *is* kind to her, but that man isn't him—that man isn't her husband.'
>
> *Dialogue No. 2*: The circumstances are the same. Again, *A* says 'Her husband is kind to her.' This time *B* says '*He* is kind to her, but *he* isn't her husband.'

In each case *B* is in possession of exactly the same facts; but he chooses to reply with different references to the pronoun 'he.' Which form of words is proper? My own intuitions are that both forms of words can, under appropriate circumstances, be proper, even though *A* is making the same mistake in both cases.

This could be explained by a general principle for pronominalization, namely that the anaphoric reference carried by a pronoun like 'he' can either be back to the previous speaker's reference (it may be one's own), *or* to the previous phrase's semantic reference. In Dialogue no. 1, *B*'s use of 'he' refers to *A*'s speaker's reference, and in Dialogue no. 2, to *A*'s semantic reference.

In the same way, when someone sees the man raking the leaves and says 'Oh, Smith is raking the leaves,' either one can reply 'He isn't raking the leaves, because that man raking the leaves isn't Smith,' or one can say 'He *is* raking the leaves, but he is not Smith.' In the first case, the 'he' refers back to the semantic reference of the previous speaker. In the second case, the 'he' refers back to the speaker's reference.

In the case of definite descriptions there may be, in fact, some preference for referring back to the speaker's reference, because the semantic reference may be unimportant, if one isn't at all concerned about the other thing (if any) which *does* fit the definite description. But I think both are legitimate: both would be proper dialogue, proper response.

If this is so, the notion of speaker's reference may have been a pragmatic one to start with, but it comes into semantics in this way. The semantics of someone's use of a pronoun may depend on a previous speaker's reference rather than on a previous semantic reference. Therefore I think it would be going too far to say that the notion of speaker's reference has little at all to do with semantics. It isn't itself a semantic notion; but it can come into the semantics of pronominalization.

Furthermore, as against an ambiguity theory, it seems to me that this example renders such a theory less plausible. For in this case not only is an ambiguity postulated where it need not have been, not only have general principles been given where the ambiguity theory doesn't give general principles, not only would the general principles have applied anyway to a hypothetical language which *didn't* have this ambiguity—not only are all these things the case, but here the ambiguity theory seems to me to run up against a difficulty, because on a particular occasion, of course, the definite description is meant in only one of the two senses. Suppose that on a given occasion it is being used referentially (or that it is being used attributively—it doesn't matter which). Then on the ambiguity view there is only one referent on this occasion, which is *both* the speaker's referent *and* the semantic referent.

Let me explain this. First, of course, the ambiguity theory too has to allow the notion of speaker's referent and semantic referent, because they are general notions that apply to all languages, so that they would apply to the ambiguous language too. It is just that the ambiguity theory has added what I would consider to be an extra idle wheel which duplicates this distinction in the following way: it makes an expression like 'the ϕ' semantically ambiguous, so that where one would say, on the other account, simply that the speaker's referent diverges from the semantic referent, one instead says that the speaker's referent is a semantic referent in this case also. So in this case, on the ambiguity theory, rather than there being two kinds of referent in a given usage, there is an ambiguity of interpretation. Once the interpretation has been settled, the speaker's referent and the semantic referent are the same. In the referential case it would be the man *you think* is drinking champagne; in the attributive case it would be the man who is actually drinking champagne. It would be the man who actually murdered Smith in the attributive case, the man *you think* murdered Smith in the referential case. So, if the ambiguity theory were correct, then in the case of 'Smith's murderer is insane' there would be only one entity that a pronoun could refer back to, since the referent of 'Smith's murderer' would be both the speaker's referent and the semantic referent.[20]

If this isn't so, as I think it isn't, and in the dialogues I have given the pronoun 'he' could be used to refer back *either* to the husband or to the man with her, this presents a problem for a view which supposes that in this conversational context there is only one referent, which in this case would have to be, I suppose, the man who is with the woman in question.

If I am right, this would be an actual case which is problematic for an ambiguity view, but not for the one I advocate here. But of course, this case is a rather specialized corner of language, and one might not want to rely on it. One might wish to rely instead on the more general arguments given above, that even if English were

---

20. Of course, in the attributive case, there may be no semantic referent; the referential case may be one where no object satisfies the description. But nevertheless there is supposed to be both a speaker's referent and a semantic referent.

postulated to satisfy Russell's theory, the phenomena described by Donnellan would still arise; that the notions of speaker's reference and semantic reference are notions we have anyway; that postulating any type of ambiguity adds an extra complication if pragmatic considerations are adequate. Relying on these considerations would leave us free, in the presence of more evidence, to change our mind and decide that an ambiguity theory is correct.

Let me sum up what I have been saying. It is argued that empty terms can sometimes have a reference in particular cases where one is talking about something, even though neither that thing nor anything else fits the definite description one uses. As against this I say, in the case both of proper names and of definite descriptions, that this is so if one is interested in speaker's reference, that is, in what one is talking about; but it is not so if one is interested in semantic reference, that is, what the name is a name of, or what the definite description refers to, in the speaker's language. In the case of the proper name, only if the speaker's general intention to use the name as a name of a given thing is satisfied, can we say that his name has reference—only if his general semantic intention is satisfied. In the case of 'the ϕ,' only if some unique thing fits the predicate 'ϕ'[21] can we say that the description has a reference in the speaker's language.

So the relevant notion, that of speaker's reference, is a pragmatic notion in the sense of being a notion about speech acts rather than about the semantics that we want to set up for the speaker's language, or for any other language. But though it is a pragmatic and not a semantic notion, it does have a certain significance for the semantics

---

21. Some might not be so sure of the uniqueness condition, which presents another issue. Sometimes, it may seem to be implied, but perhaps not always, so one might say simply 'only if something fits the predicate ϕ.' In the case where you explicitly imply uniqueness, as when you say 'the *only* thing having ϕ,' one would have exactly Russell's conditions, but one problem for the strict Russellian is why 'only' doesn't always sound redundant. However, sometimes, I would add, 'the' certainly does imply uniqueness.

of pronominalization. So it enters into semantics, so to speak, by the back door, because of rules for back reference of pronouns. But though this is so, and though this gives the notion a greater semantic importance, on the other hand it creates even more difficulties for this view that I was opposing, that is, the view that it is part of the semantics of the language that this kind of ambiguity can occur. I therefore conclude—this is a little conclusion from a long discussion!—that, by contrast with the other two cases cited in the beginning of this lecture, we do not here have a third kind of case where what were classically thought to be empty terms really have reference. At least we don't have such a case if by 'reference' we mean *reference in the semantics of the language.*[22]

---

22. In Kripke (1977) I suggested that considerations analogous to those I apply to Donnellan might also apply to what various writers have written about indefinite descriptions (Kripke 2011a: 124). For an attempt to carry out such a suggestion, see Ludlow and Neale (1991).

December 4, 1973

Last time I discussed mostly a view of Donnellan's to the effect that empty singular descriptions can sometimes have reference. In the course of this I developed a methodological apparatus for consideration of these questions, which I think has its own intrinsic interest—namely, a means to test a claim to have refuted a semantical theory by appeal to certain phenomena. Imagine a hypothetical language in which it is *stipulated* that this semantical theory applies, then test whether that hypothetical language would exhibit the linguistic phenomena you think cast doubt on the theory. This is really, of course, the same test as should have been applied in consideration of the English language itself, but it will somehow psychologically have the effect of one's being less quick to draw a conclusion from certain linguistic phenomena that a certain theory doesn't apply, by saying 'Oh, well, so we see that this theory isn't true of English.' Instead we see of what language the theory *would* be true, and whether that language would in the alleged way diverge from English; and the results may not be what we think. My discussion of Donnellan was supposed to illustrate this device.

Before moving on, let me make a couple of remarks related to Donnellan's paper. First I will mention one more point specifically on Donnellan himself, since it is a rather popular one. It is advocated, for example, in Partee (1970) and I believe in Stalnaker (1972). This view says that Donnellan's distinction between referential and attributive uses should be used to analyze the familiar distinction between *de dicto* and *de re*. Now, I have recognized Donnellan's distinction in the previous lecture, though I have denied that it is a semantic one or creates any case for an ambiguity. I would if I had time argue that this distinction is neither exclusive nor exhaustive and admits of overlapping and borderline cases; but I won't do this here, beyond emphasizing one important point. To suppose that the distinction is exhaustive is one of the mistakes, I think, that Donnellan makes. Unlike Russell and Frege, he does not consider indirect discourse reports at all. One might suppose, naively, that in reports on what a speaker has said, the person making the indirect discourse report also uses the description referentially or attributively, and must use it the same way as the speaker does. This seems to me quite false: she is generally doing neither. If I say that Jones says that the greatest logician in the world is tall, I am neither referentially nor attributively talking about the greatest logician in the world. I am just reporting what Jones says. I may not even believe that there is any such person, but only that Jones does. I may not think there is a unique greatest logician; I may even think (replace 'logician' by 'mind reader') that the predicate involved is empty.

What about the *de re* case, as in 'Jones believes *of* the greatest logician in the world that he is tall'? Russell, as we know, would have analyzed this locution in terms of his notion of the scope of a definite description.[1] But just as the inner scope reading has nothing to do with Donnellan's attributive use (and indeed the distinction is really inapplicable here), so the *de re* reading has nothing to do with Donnellan's referential use. Now the referential-attributive distinction does apply, but the *de dicto* case may be either one. A speaker may think that some particular person is the greatest logician in the

1. Quine (1956) brings out the distinction in another way, as a syntactic one taken primitively. Readers of his paper seem to have forgotten about Russell's theory of the distinction. For some other current work of my own on these issues, see Kripke (2005) as well as Kripke (2011c).

world, and think that Jones believes of him that he is tall; this would
be referential. However, this need not be the case. The speaker may,
for example, have no idea who the greatest logician in the world
might be, but does think that (for some reason) Jones is someone
who thinks that the leading people in academic fields are invariably
tall, and also that he believes some particular person to be the
world's greatest logician. (Without having necessarily met him, he
assumes him to be tall.) Then the speaker would think that Jones
believes, of the greatest logician in the world, that he is tall. But the
speaker's use here of 'the greatest logician in the world' is attributive.
He has no particular person in mind, other than 'the world's greatest
logician,' to determine the reference of the description.

So it would be quite wrong to apply this distinction to the case
of indirect discourse, or to any other case of *de dicto* and *de re* which
is ordinarily analyzed by the notion of scope,[2] and we don't have an
independent argument for the distinction here. Whatever arguments there are for the distinction come from other areas, and
it should not be applied to this case. One can apply it only by
confusing what the speaker may have in mind with what Jones,
the person he is talking about, may have in mind, and these are not
the same.

One interesting point about speaker's reference which I will
mention, because it is connected with my remarks on proper names
in *N&N*, is this: just as the semantic reference of a name may be
transmitted from one speaker to another by links in a chain, so, presumably, this is true of the speaker's reference of a description. For
example, the man in the corner of the room drinking champagne
may later come to be suspected of a murder. If he is not otherwise
identified, the description may spread from one person to another,

2. Or by Quine's analysis in Quine (1956), as mentioned in the previous note.

even though it may not fit the person supposedly identified. The speaker's reference is then transmitted from link to link in a chain, just as semantic reference is. One may be specifying the person one is talking about as the same person that was being talked about by the community from which one heard certain notions about that person, and so on, going back and back. It is unlikely that this chain will be very long in the case of a mere speaker's reference, but it is possible: in particular it could happen where the speaker's reference diverges from the semantic reference in the case of a definite description.

Another case which may arise is that a speaker's referent of a proper name becomes so habitual that it becomes the semantic referent in the mouth of some community of speakers. Remember that I distinguished between a speaker's *general intentions*, as determining the semantic reference, and his *specific intentions* on a specific occasion, as determining the speaker's referent. What started out as a new speaker's referent might become habitual practice of the speaker, who adopts it again and again. The speaker may have started out by mistaking one man for another, but the practice may become so habitual that it might over time be called the "general intention" of the speaker. It might be suggested that in some of these cases the speaker's referent then takes over and becomes the semantic referent. If this becomes so in a wide enough community, a linguistic change has occurred. And I think, without being able to elaborate on it at this point, that this may have a great deal to do with the solution of various problems about when linguistic change can occur in the reference of proper names, although the speaker doesn't explicitly intend to start a new practice. This is a problem which various people have raised for me at various times, and it is a rather delicate problem. And the hypothetical case just described may be important for understanding some of the cases where such a change can occur.

An example is Gareth Evans's well-known case of 'Madagascar' (Evans 1973; see also Kripke 1972/1980: 93, 96–97, 163), similar to my own case of 'Santa Claus.'[3] According to Evans, 'Madagascar' (actually, apparently, something similar) was originally a name of part of mainland Africa, but Marco Polo mistakenly used it, thinking he was following African usage, as a name for the island we call 'Madagascar' today. Then originally, there was a speaker's reference, but not a semantic reference. Eventually, when it became habitual to call the island 'Madagascar,' one could only pronounce the reference semantically correct.[4]

Let me now make the following remarks. Since I may in the last lecture have given the impression—though apparently I didn't to at least one of the questioners—that I wish to defend Russell down the line on the issue of definite descriptions, I will say something about where I think that doubts about Russell's theory may arise.

3. In *N&N* (Kripke 1972/1980: 163) I am probably basing my comments on an earlier version of Evans (1973) I heard read at a workshop, since I describe it as using the Madagascar example to defend a description theory, whereas that does not seem just to the final version of Evans's paper.

4. This story is the impression one would probably get from what Evans says. However, I have looked up several references regarding the name 'Madagascar' and Marco Polo, and I am quite doubtful on the basis of these that the story is the right one. Marco Polo never visited the island, and others may have misunderstood what place he was talking about. (Maybe he was actually "baptizing" some place. Later Portuguese explorers called the island by another name, 'São Lourenço' [St. Lawrence], and only later was it discovered that this was the same place as the island Madagascar.) It doesn't matter what really happened, as long as it could have, and I suppose indeed it could have. I do suppose that my earlier case of St. Nicholas and Santa Claus is a genuine case of a shift from a historical saint to a mythical character.

Misunderstandings need not lead to a reference shift in any ordinary sense. The indri (ironically, a lemur native to Madagascar!) was mistakenly so-called by the French naturalist Pierre Sonnerat, thinking he was following native usage. Actually, in Malagasy, 'indri' meant 'look' or something like that. There is no original reference, or speaker's reference, in this case. Sonnerat might be regarded as an initial baptizer, who erroneously thought he was following native usage. It is also called 'babakoto,' the true native name. (This example was introduced into the philosophical literature by David Lewis, who told it to Quine. It is found in the dictionaries that I have. However, it is questioned by Hacking (1981), including the accuracy of the account just given of Malagasy usage.)

They may arise precisely—at least the way Russell is usually defended—in the way transmission of speaker's reference can be involved in the use of a definite description. Many have said, against Russell, that definite descriptions can be used even when the uniqueness condition is not fulfilled. If someone says 'The table is pretty,' or 'Bring the table over here,' she of course is not implying that there is only one table in the universe. And this seems to be true.

The orthodox Russellian reply is that the speaker must have some other predicates in mind that she could add on, and which would fill out the phrase 'the table.' It might be 'the table in that corner of the room' or 'the table having such-and-such other characteristics.' And the additional characteristics are understood by both speaker and hearer.[5]

Considerations about speaker's reference and semantic reference apply to another case which is used both in defense of Russell and against him in the literature. This is the case of indefinite descriptions and anaphoric uses of phrases such as 'the table.' One feature of definite descriptions in English is that in almost every case where one can make a back reference by a pronoun ('almost' is required as a slight hedge because of at least one example) one could use a definite description instead. If one says 'A man was walking on the beach and he picked up a can' one could instead have said 'A man was walking on the beach and *the* man picked up a can.' Here of course one certainly is not implying there was only one man in the universe. And no additional predicate has been given to show which

---

5. Since this was said, I have had the benefit of seeing Stephen Neale's analysis in Neale (1990; see especially section 3.7). He points out that ordinary quantifiers, such as 'everyone' in 'Everyone got sick last night,' are similarly plainly intended to be restricted to a limited portion of the human race. Neale also points out that alternatives to adding explicit restrictions might be considered, as in the case at hand. So I may have been too pessimistic in Kripke (1977) regarding this problem. See, however, Ostertag (1998; section VI of the introduction, pp. 25–27, and the notes), that may reinstate my original pessimism, though with qualifications.

man was meant. One may, therefore, think that both Russell's analysis of indefinite descriptions and his analysis of definite descriptions have been refuted, because surely when one says 'A man was walking on the beach and *the* man did such and such' the analysis should be this: when I say 'a man' I have a definite man in mind who is being referred to by the phrase 'a man'; 'the man,' or 'he,' simply carries the same reference back.

This is a question which has been much debated in both the philosophical and the linguistic literature. Can an indefinite description such as 'a man' be analyzed simply as an existential quantifier or should one rather say that it must be regarded, at least in some cases, as a referring expression, somewhat like a name, which refers to a particular person of whom one is talking? In the philosophical literature, Strawson, for example, notably argues that 'a man' must refer in a sense (Strawson 1952), and there is a more recent paper by Charles Chastain which elaborates this view (Chastain 1975).[6]

The usual reply from the existential quantification point of view to this has been something like this: if you say 'A man walked on the beach and *the* man picked up a stone' one can just regard this as a very long existential quantification: 'There is an x such that x is a man and x walked on the beach and x picked up a stone':

1. $(\exists x)(x$ is a man $\land x$ walked on the beach $\land x$ picked up a stone)

Here '*the* man' is to signal that we repeat the same variable that was used in the existential quantifier before. It is in fact no objection to Russell to say that there isn't a unique man here: one can analyze the

---

6. See also Strawson (1952). Chastain introduces the term 'anaphoric chain' to express this idea. The indefinite description gives the initial reference and subsequent definite descriptions are anaphoric on it.

omitted predicate as simply being that of being identical with x. This is something that might be ignored in some discussions. But of course a Russellian definite description can itself contain variables, and they can be bound by previous quantifiers: so why not here? 'The man' then becomes 'the y such that y is a man and $y = x$,' where x is the variable being bound by the initial existential quantifier. And one might say in support of this, as against the other view, that one has precisely the same uses of 'he' and 'the man' in cases where there is no definite person we have in mind. For example, 'If any man poaches on my land *he* will be executed,' or 'If any man poaches on my land *the* man will be executed.' Here one doesn't have any definite man in mind that one is referring to, but the use of 'the man' simply carries forward the variable which occurs in the initial quantification.[7]

Unfortunately this won't really handle all of the cases. One can say 'A man walked on the beach and he picked up a stone.' Someone else may reply 'No, he didn't pick up a stone.' The man who says that in reply to the first speaker thinks that he is contradicting him, but on the view in question, how can his remarks be analyzed so that this intuition is preserved? Well, the existential analysis of indefinite followed by definite should be 'there is an x such that x is a man and x walked on the beach and x didn't pick up a stone.'

The trouble with this is, of course, that it doesn't contradict the first statement at all. Both of them may well be true. It may well be the case that one man walked on the beach and did pick up a stone and another man walked on the beach and *didn't* pick up a stone. And people like Geach who have defended all such uses of 'he' as simply picking up a previous variable in this way can't analyze this kind of case (Geach 1962). The two statements they give

7. Similarly, 'Mary believed that a man was on the beach and the man/he. . . .' Mary's belief need not be true, so no reference to a particular man need be implied.

will not contradict each other. This applies even more clearly in Strawson's case:

> A: A man fell over the edge.
> B: He didn't fall; he jumped.

(Strawson 1952: 187)

What can be said about this? How can the reply be regarded as a contradiction of what the first man said? The first man's remark could be analyzed as 'There is an x such that x is a man and x fell over the edge':

$$2. \ (\exists x)(\mathrm{Man}(x) \wedge \mathrm{Fell}(x))$$

Now B comments: 'He didn't fall: he jumped.' What is the analysis of that? Well, analogously: 'There is an x such that x is a man and x jumped (rather than falling)':

$$3. \ (\exists x)(\mathrm{Man}(x) \wedge \mathrm{Jumped}(x))$$

It is very plain that these two statements don't contradict each other. Of course one can make the man in question more definite by putting 'fell over the edge' into this second statement too; but that isn't very good because then the speaker's reply will be an out-and-out contradiction. So one might think that everything is against the existential analysis here, and that everything is against any Russellian analysis of definite descriptions as well.

This doesn't really follow. I will say, though, that those who have advocated the view that in some cases 'A man walked on the beach' has a singular term in it, 'a man,' which refers, have generally not emphasized this contradiction kind of case, which I think is probably the best for their purposes. (The case that Strawson gives is a contradiction, but he doesn't emphasize that it is a contradiction.)

The mere fact that one can pick up a pronoun and go on with 'he' or 'the man'—this is all that is usually pointed out—is very little evidence in and of itself. This could also happen if we began with 'if *any* man poaches on my land . . .,' which seems plainly not to refer to a particular man, and to carry some generality.

But one might, if one wished to defend the existential analysis, take a line like the following. First, the singular term analysis of 'A man walked on the beach' would make it false—and this is, for example, explicitly stated by Chastain (1975)—to say 'A man walked on the beach,' if the man you had in mind wasn't walking on the beach.[8] 'A man' is supposed to refer to the man the speaker has in mind—call him Jones—so 'A man walked on the beach' must be at least materially equivalent to 'Jones walked on the beach,' and the statement will be false if Jones did not walk on the beach. This doesn't seem quite correct to my ear. If someone says 'A man walked on the beach,' and the man he had in mind *wasn't* walking on the beach, one could say to him 'Well, a man *did* walk on the beach, but not the man you had in mind.' But it would seem quite incorrect to say: 'No, that is wrong. What you said is false.'

So it would seem to me that some compromise ought to be struck; or perhaps one ought not to call it a compromise. One might save the existential analysis in the following kind of way (and I think this is peculiar to some terms, like 'a man'). One might say that it is a convention, once again, for pronominalization, or for use of 'the man,' that if one has an existential quantification, and there is a particular person who is held in mind as cashing that in (that is, a speaker's referent—on this occasion the speaker's referent of 'a man,' which is the thing he thinks makes his existential quantification

---

8. Chastain in one place does acknowledge that purely existential cases of indefinite descriptions may occur (1975: 212). But for what he regards as a typical use where an indefinite description does refer and begins an anaphoric chain, his view appears to be what I attribute to him.

true), then this can be referred back to with a pronoun, either by the speaker himself or by any later speaker. And one can say such things as 'No—he didn't fall: he jumped.' One isn't then trying to use the initial speaker's existential quantification, because one may not by so doing contradict what the first speaker has said. One's statement wouldn't be a contrary of what he has said; it would be just another existential quantification which might well be true even though the first statement was also true. But if instead one uses the pronominalization device that I mentioned in the last lecture, this difficulty is avoided. Recall that I allow a pronoun to refer to the speaker's reference in a dialogue. In this case, analogously, it could refer to the thing the speaker has in mind when using the indefinite description. It does justice to the intuition that if the speaker has some particular man in mind, that man can be referred back to in a dialogue as 'he,' while allowing us to preserve the existential analysis.

This suggestion may appear obvious once it is made; at least it does to me. I think that actually there may be other problems as well: all the same, it is strange that it doesn't seem to be taken up by either side of the dispute in the literature. One side of the dispute always says that one is carrying through the same variable that one starts with; the other side says that one has a singular term which is referring to some definite person, and that in this case the existential analysis must be falsified. Neither needs to be the case. One could simply adopt the position which makes it a matter of semantic reference and speaker's reference.

I am going to go over the allotted time in this lecture, as I expected. So I will just simply do so, so as to get a chance to finish. This concludes the sketchy things I have to say about these notions. The most important one, to do with how a speaker's reference might become a semantic reference, is one which I only stated in a sentence. But I want to talk about what I promised.

What I promised to talk about in this lecture was the final problem of negative existentials. The thing which has most boggled people, and confuses me still to this day, is how to analyze a singular negative existential statement. The problem becomes more acute rather than less so, on my view. Why do I say that? The original problem is: what can someone mean when he says that Sherlock Holmes does not exist? Is he talking of a definite thing, and saying of it that it doesn't exist? The reason the problem becomes somewhat more acute on my view is that it has been universally regarded in the literature as unproblematic to make a negative existential statement using a predicate. 'There are no leopards in the Arctic'—this simply asserts the emptiness of a certain predicate. Similarly 'There are no unicorns'—that is absolutely fine (I have seen it given as an example). Not according to me, because what I say is that, just as there is no definite person, Sherlock Holmes, to whom non-existence is being attributed, so there is no definite property, that of being a unicorn, which is being asserted to have empty extension in the statement 'There are no unicorns.' And, of course, part of the resistance one might feel to what I suggested about unicorns is on account of just that. If there isn't some kind of possible animal which is being asserted not to have instances in the actual world, what does one mean when one says 'There are no unicorns'?

This *is* a problem. But it shouldn't lead to resistance to my view of unicorns. For it is surely just as legitimate to say 'There are no bandersnatches.' One might say this to a child who asked to be taken to see a bandersnatch in the zoo after reading the poem in question. But here on almost anyone's picture, surely not just my own, there is no definite kind of animal called 'the bandersnatch' which is being asserted not to have instances in the actual world. The poet was just making up an animal. The only thing we are told about bandersnatches is that they are 'frumious,' whatever that means. It is also implied that they are dangerous; or should be 'shunned.' Surely no one would think that one can say what kind of animal a bandersnatch *would* have been had there been bandersnatches, what kind of species is being asserted to be empty when one denies that there are any bandersnatches. Yet one can tell one's little child that there are no bandersnatches.

So the problem really is just as acute for predicates of a certain kind, those introduced by fictional names of species, as it is for singular terms. But people have concentrated on and worried themselves to death over the case of a singular term, because only there did they have the feeling that the object must exist, so that one can say of it that it doesn't exist.

Two suggestions immediately come to mind.[9] These suggestions arise out of what I myself have already said. Before presenting them, let me remark that there are, in the case of the singular existential statement, really two very different kinds of cases. They are assimilated in the literature but they are certainly different. First, one may use a genuine name and, truly or falsely, say of the object that it exists. For example, I say 'Napoleon really existed' or 'Napoleon didn't really exist' (I say that falsely). In this case, as I have emphasized before, contrary to Frege and Russell it seems to me to be clear that one is quite legitimately talking about the object, quite legitimately saying of it that it exists. It is possible that it would not have: Napoleon would not have existed had his parents never met. That does not mean something about the deeds of Napoleon not having been performed, or some other predicate about Napoleon not having been satisfied, had his parents never met. For all I know any famous

9. Well, a third one does too, namely the view of Frege and Russell, but I take it that I have disposed of that. If I haven't, I am not going to convince anyone on the other side at this point; and if I have, I already have.

deeds of Napoleon would still have occurred, any predicate in question would have been satisfied, even if his parents had never met, and maybe satisfied *better* by someone else. This is not what is in question when one says that, though Napoleon existed, he might not have existed. And if someone thinks falsely—as the logician Whately, with tongue in cheek, pretended to do—that Napoleon doesn't exist, Napoleon himself can quite correctly say to him 'So you thought that I didn't exist, did you?,' and send him, perhaps quite correctly, to an appropriate place. 'Napoleon might not have existed' is as much a statement about Napoleon as any other that predicates a genuine property of him. There may be some sense in which existence isn't a predicate, in which one can say that 'Napoleon exists' doesn't attribute a property to Napoleon. After all, you are not attributing a property to Napoleon when you say he exists— you are saying there is such a thing for properties to be attributed to. That in some rather obscure sense seems to me to be true, and it is perhaps what Kant had in mind. But it should not be understood as implying that when one says 'Napoleon exists' one isn't saying something *about* Napoleon, or isn't using 'Napoleon' as a singular term just as much here as in any other case. On the contrary, there is a fact that there is such a thing as that thing—Napoleon—and there might not have been any such thing.[10]

Quite different (and this is one of the additional problems which then arises, on my view) is the case where an empty name is used. For one surely is not saying anything, or so it seems at first blush, *about* Sherlock Holmes when one says (apparently about Sherlock Holmes) that Sherlock Holmes doesn't exist. And if someone falsely believes that Sherlock Holmes does really exist—that is, the man in the story—there is no possible entity, let alone an actual one, who

10. See Moore (1959b: 126), discussed in Lecture II.

can come up to that person and say 'Huh, you thought I existed, did you?' the way Napoleon could in the other case.

What then is the solution to the problem? It seems that in some sense the analysis of a singular existence statement will depend on whether that statement is true. And this, of course, seems in and of itself to be absolutely intolerable: the analysis of a statement should not depend on its truth-value. Or so at any rate might be our prejudice.[11] Nevertheless, one shouldn't ignore the facts here, and the facts seem to me to be as I have stated.

Quite analogous remarks could be made, to some extent, about predicates, except that here there are negative existentials with empty predicates which are unproblematic (unlike the unicorn and bandersnatch cases). For example, one might truly, I suppose, say that there are no giraffes in the Arctic. 'Giraffe in the Arctic Circle' is an ordinary predicate which happens to have an empty extension. That case is fine. But 'There are no unicorns' raises problems analogous to the bandersnatch case, in my view.

Two things I said come to mind. One of them is to use the apparatus of fictional characters which I developed before. Why not say that when one says 'Hamlet does not exist' one is speaking of a fictional character? Perhaps many people might think that that is what I want to say. But it can't be right, taken straightforwardly, because one isn't saying *of* a fictional character that it doesn't exist. On the contrary, the fictional character does exist. So the *fictional character* is not something which is being said not to exist. If you say that the fictional character didn't exist, you would be wrongly assimilating this case to the case of Moloch, where one can say truly, as I did before, there was no such god as Moloch, that Moloch didn't exist.

---

11. This is related to what Geach (1962) has called "Buridan's Law," but it is simpler and even less apt to be at all questionable.

That is in contrast with the case of Hamlet, rather than being the same kind of case. If one wishes to talk about the fictional character, one should say that it *does* exist.

One should bear in mind here that one should not confuse levels of language. Where I said originally that an empty name was just a pretense, as in the case of 'Hamlet,' or a mistake, as in the case of 'Vulcan' (where one thought a name had been properly introduced when it had not), that was one level of language. An extended level of language was set up by the introduction of an ontology of fictional characters, or legendary objects; and this level uses just the same names for them as were originally empty. This happens especially in the case of pretense in fiction. But one shouldn't confuse this level of language with the previous one. One should not say that, when an author is just pretending to refer to a man though she is not, that that pretense was in and of itself naming a fictional character. One should say that she was *creating* a fictional character.

It is true that because of the extended use of language these levels often get elided. One might say just 'Hamlet is not real: he is merely a fictional character' (which can be analyzed as 'Hamlet is not a real person: he is a fictional person') just as one might say 'This is not a real duck: it is a toy duck.' One can say that with perfect propriety when one is talking about an ordinary object. But one might even say 'Hamlet doesn't exist: Hamlet is merely a *fictional* character.' Here—though one might well be tempted to make assertions of this kind—one is really mixing kinds of discourse. For after all it isn't the *fictional* character which does not exist; there *is* such a fictional character. (Again, contrast the case of Moloch who, on the premises previously mentioned, doesn't exist even in the sense that a mythological god does exist.) In saying 'Hamlet doesn't exist: Hamlet is merely a fictional character' one is really saying, first, that there is no such *person* as Hamlet—that on that level of language there is no referent for the name. But then, just because there is no referent for the name, this work in front of us is a work of fiction; so therefore (one is saying) there *is* such a fictional character as Hamlet. There is such a fictional character just because there is no such *person*, though a name purporting to refer to such a person does occur in a work of fiction.

One might think that the ontology of fictional characters would be of some help—that when one is referring to a fictional character, the denial of existence might be a (somewhat strange) way of saying that the character is only fictional. But on the contrary, 'Hamlet does not exist; Hamlet is only a fictional character,' only illustrates the problem of interpretation. The first half purports to say that something does not exist. But the second half uses 'Hamlet' to refer to something that *does* actually exist (in virtue of the existence of a certain play). It appears that 'Hamlet' must be construed ambiguously here, even though the second half of the sentence purports to explain the first.[12]

I am very suspicious of a view that takes the denial of existence to mean 'fictional' or 'not real.' First, when one says 'Suppose Moses had never existed' or 'Suppose Napoleon had never existed,' one doesn't mean by this 'Suppose Moses (Napoleon) had been a mere fictional character.' One doesn't mean that at all. Napoleon couldn't have been a mere fictional character, any more than he could have been a prime number. There might have

---

12. Romina Padró has suggested to me that it may be possible to draw an analogy here with cases of the toy-duck fallacy, and use it to account for negative existentials. Statements such as 'Hamlet does not exist, he is only a fictional character,' would be, on this view, a way of saying that Hamlet is not a real person but a real fictional character. Analogously, the toy duck is not a real duck, but it is a real toy duck. One might emphasize this when speaking to a child who is fantasizing about having a real pet duck. (This connects with her remark that when locutions such as 'That's a duck' refer to a toy duck, they may be introducing a fictional context. See Kripke (2011c: 346, note 62).)

been a fictional work written about someone who performed just the same exploits as Napoleon; but that doesn't mean that Napoleon *himself* would, under such circumstances, have been a mere fictional character.

Second, the additional thing which makes me suspicious of this view (I actually think that the remark about Napoleon is fairly conclusive against it, but here is something which is another initial source of suspicion) is that it just seems to me that if, as I said, the introduction of the ontology of fictional characters is an extended use of language, then singular existential statements (and denials thereof) could have been made even if this extension had not existed. Even if we didn't have an ontology of fictional characters in our language, one could still say with perfect propriety that there was no such person as Hamlet. One doesn't need some extra kind of entity, or so it would seem intuitively, just to say that.

Finally, we not only have fictional characters but also fictional fictional characters. In that case, of course, a special signal would have to be given, because one wishes to distinguish real fictional characters from merely fictional fictional characters like Gonzago. One wishes to say that such a fictional character as Hamlet does exist, and such a fictional character as Gonzago does not. So perhaps one first gives a sortal, and then uses 'exist' to say whether something is a real member of that sortal. For example, if the sortal is 'person,' then on this view one uses 'exist' to mean that something is a real person, rather than a fictional one. But the sortal could be 'fictional person,' and then one would be contrasting real fictional persons (such as Hamlet) with fictional fictional ones (such as Gonzago). However, this would be a quite misleading use of 'exist,' because all such entities could be said to exist in the ordinary sense (assuming both concrete and abstract objects exist). But in this proposal one would be saying what kind of entity they were by speaking of whether they existed or not. And this it seems to me to be *prima facie* unacceptable.[13]

Even in cases where language is in fact very reluctant to apply the notion of *fictional character*, we can still say 'A does not exist.' I think I have mentioned in the question period the case of Sam Jones and the check, in which I, lying to the restaurant owner, say that Sam Jones will come to pay the check. One might be very reluctant to speak of a fictional character here, if that is all I have said. But the police could very well comment on what I have said by saying 'Sam Jones doesn't exist.'

So it seems to me that the singular existential statement should not be analyzed as using a predicate which isn't really existence, but which divides one kind of entity from another. I emphasize this because some might have taken me to be attempting just such an analysis, given this whole ontology of fictional characters I have recognized.

Another suggestion might be a metalinguistic analysis. After all, when someone says that there are no bandersnatches, doesn't he mean that the predicate 'is a bandersnatch' doesn't apply to any kind of animal, or something like that—something metalinguistic about the predicate? And if someone says 'Vulcan doesn't exist,' he just means that 'Vulcan' is an empty name. So why not analyze these statements metalinguistically?

---

13. Various people have been attracted to the suggestion that while the pretense in fiction is to refer to say, a person, one is really referring to a fictional character (see for example Salmon 1987, 1998, and 2002). And similarly for myth, though here one would have to attribute a false belief as to the referent, as opposed to the real ones. Since on this theory there are no empty fictional or mythological names, there seems to be a consequence of it that even the earliest people knew, implicitly or otherwise, about the ontologies of mythological characters. But that of course seems implausible. Compare this to the case of modern set-theoretic analyses of the natural numbers. Did even Frege wish to claim that his analysis was what we meant all along?

One problem about this might seem to be that, once again, it doesn't apply to a counterfactual use. If I say 'Vulcan does not exist' it may seem that what I say amounts to 'The name "Vulcan" is empty.' But I surely wouldn't count, counterfactually, just any old case in which the name 'Vulcan' *did* have a reference as a case in which Vulcan would have existed. Much less, in the case of a real name, would I say that Moses does exist, but that if the name 'Moses' hadn't been used as a name, Moses wouldn't have existed. This seems quite inadequate. In the case, in fact, where a man is really being named, as in the case of Moses, it does seem that when one says 'Suppose Moses wouldn't have existed,' or 'Consider circumstances in which Moses didn't exist,' one doesn't mean 'Consider a case in which the name "Moses" didn't have any reference.' That might have happened even if he *had* existed, and no one had been named 'Moses.'

One might say 'Well, all right, in the empty case anyway we mean something metalinguistic, even when speaking counterfactually.' But this once again yields the problem of giving two analyses, depending on whether a statement is true or false. That is, we have to distinguish between the case where the name really is in fact empty, and the case where it isn't.

One might say that at least we can patch it up in the empty case. It is true that a case where the name 'Vulcan' was merely used as a name of something or other wouldn't thereby be a case where Vulcan really existed. But that is not what we have in mind. After all, the name 'Vulcan,' like any proper name in English, is probably used for any number of objects, so that one ought to refer not just to the term 'Vulcan' itself but to a particular use of it. When one says 'Vulcan does not exist,' pointing to a page in the writings of some deluded astronomer, one means 'That use of the name has no referent'; and to suppose that the *name* 'Vulcan' could have been used as a name for something else is not to suppose that *that* use of the name *would* have had a referent. Of course, a book just like the one in question could have had the name 'Vulcan' in it, used in a way such that it had a referent; but one might try, in some manner which is not entirely clear to me, though its flavor is clear enough, to say that we won't count it as *that* (originally mentioned) use of the name unless, let's say, the entire history (on my view) was the same; at least, enough of it should be the same for us to be able to say that this hypothetical use goes back to the same kind of referent as the other use, and here it goes back to nothing.

Nevertheless, this kind of metalinguistic analysis, like any other, seems to me to be beset by difficulties. Suppose one runs across either the name 'Vulcan' or the name 'Santa Claus.' One is an anthropologist, and one sees the name 'Vulcan' or 'Santa Claus' on a printed page, and one asks 'Is that a name?' Someone might answer, 'No, that name has no referent.' This is quite different from what one is telling the child, who is now getting grown up, when one says 'Look, Santa Claus doesn't really exist.' If one is able to tell the child that, the child must have learned something about Santa Claus. He isn't really just being told that some name, which he may otherwise not understand at all, has no referent, nor even that in a particular use it has no referent. If he comes to believe that Santa Claus does not exist, and expresses this belief afterwards by saying 'Santa Claus does not exist,' he is using the name and not mentioning it. If he were merely mentioning it he would be in the same position as the anthropologist. For the anthropologist can certainly learn that the name 'Santa Claus' has no referent: that is easy. But the anthropologist may not learn thereby what the child learns—that Santa Claus doesn't exist. In fact, even though he is grown up, he may still believe in Santa Claus, referring to him by a different name, of course, or even referring to him by the same name but thinking: 'Oh, well, that kid must be using the term "Santa Claus" differently, since *he* uses the term "Santa Claus" with no referent.'

Things get even worse if one tries to analyze indirect discourse in this way. Suppose someone says 'The Greeks believed that there was such a divine being as Zeus,' or that 'Zeus existed.' Well, what are we saying that the Greeks believed? On the analysis in question we are saying that the Greeks believed that the name 'Zeus' had a referent. This I suppose is true in this particular case, but it is true only because the Greeks used the same name as we. For all we know, when we say 'The Greeks believed that Zeus existed,' it may be the case that the Greeks either used a different name, or that they didn't use any name at all. And we are not prejudging this question when we say that the Greeks believed that Zeus existed. Or if we say that such and such an atheistic Greek believed that Zeus didn't exist, again we don't mean that this atheistic Greek believed that the name 'Zeus' had no referent. He too may not have used the name 'Zeus,' or may not have used any name at all.

One can't even analyze the first statement with safety as 'The Greeks believed that some name with the same reference as "Zeus" designated an existing entity.' This actually compounds the problem even more, rather than helping matters. For one has first to give an analysis of the statement 'Zeus exists,' and then just report it after the 'that' as the content of the Greek's belief. As in: 'There is some name with the same reference as "Zeus" and the Greeks believed its referent existed.' One can't, so to speak, move this content outside the scope of the belief context. (Besides, does 'Zeus doesn't exist' mean *some name with the same reference as 'Zeus' has no reference*? What could that mean?) So, on this analysis, to say that the Greeks believed that Zeus exists is merely to say that the Greeks believed that some name with the same reference as 'Zeus' has a referent. But of course the Greeks, if they had never heard of the name 'Zeus,' also didn't have any belief which can be analyzed as: *some name with the same referent as the name 'Zeus' has a referent.* Once again, they may never have heard of the name 'Zeus.'

These being the problems, and my general prejudice being against supposing that a metalinguistic analysis is hidden in an ordinary statement, I felt that this approach ought to be dropped. It wouldn't work, in any case, where one is really using a non-empty name. Even where one is using an empty name, it seems an important objection that the name is being used rather than mentioned.

I have a certain tendency at this point to throw up my hands. Perhaps one shouldn't try and give an analysis at all. But instead I'll try and say how, as far as I can guess, this kind of statement got into our discourse. It does seem to me to be a genuine and unsolved problem—perhaps the most difficult in the area.

It is true, of course, that when someone knows who Santa Claus is, then he will believe that Santa Claus doesn't exist if, and only if, the name 'Santa Claus' has no referent. He would say that right off the bat. That is not to say, though, that all he means by 'Santa Claus doesn't exist' is that the name 'Santa Claus' has no referent. The latter statement could be understood by someone who has no idea what the name 'Santa Claus' is supposed to denote, only that it has no reference (in that sense it is weaker).

Those of you who stayed for the question period after the very first lecture may remember one question which I will now mention again, since anyone who heard what I said then has probably forgotten it. 'How do I analyze,' so it might go, '"The Greeks believed that Zeus was a mighty god"?' (Here I am reporting on the belief of the Greeks, who thought they were talking about a real god.) Or how do I analyze, if someone, Jones, say, reads a story and mistakenly thinks the characters in it are real, the statement that Jones believes that Sherlock Holmes is a brilliant detective (he mistakenly believes that Holmes is real)? If after all 'Sherlock Holmes' is just a pretended name, then the whole proposition which is supposed to be the content of Jones's belief is only a pretended proposition. Perhaps he merely believes that he has a belief.

One could answer this, actually, using the ontology of fictional characters, by saying that he has mistaken a fictional object for a real one. But one can give the following kind of vague answer which is independent of that, and which is needed, for example, for such cases as 'The story has it that Sherlock Holmes is a great detective.' What is it that the story has it that? There is supposed to be no such proposition as that Sherlock Holmes is a great detective which the story has it that. I said of this, not that some metalinguistic analysis should be introduced (any more than in the other cases), but that one should speak of a kind of proposition which is being asserted to exist and to be true. The story has it that there is a true proposition about Sherlock Holmes, namely that he is a great detective. An astronomer who thought that Vulcan was red would believe, first, that there is an object, Vulcan (I guess the one causing the perturbations of Mercury), which he uses the name 'Vulcan' to mention; and second, there is a proposition, which I would call a proposition *about* Vulcan, namely the proposition about Vulcan that it is red.

This is a little obscure to me, and perhaps to you. I want to be careful here, as in the other cases, to be using these names rather than mentioning them. So that in the sentence 'The astronomer believes that there is a proposition about Vulcan, saying of Vulcan that it is red,' the phrase 'about Vulcan' is a special sort of quasi-intensional use. And I should emphasize that I am going into an area about which I have little confidence, except that I prefer my view of it to anything else.

One can sloppily view the statement in question as metalinguistic, by saying that it means that the astronomer believes that the sentence 'Vulcan is red' expresses a true proposition. But that doesn't seem to me really to express the content of it. It is subject to the same kind of difficulties as the metalinguistic analysis is elsewhere. So: the astronomer believes that there is a true proposition about Vulcan, that it is red. He is wrong, not because the proposition is false but because there is no such true proposition. Nevertheless, first, it is quite plainly correct to call him wrong, in some sense, when he says that Vulcan is red, because he believes wrongly that there is a true proposition which he expresses by the words 'Vulcan is red.' Second, one might, though this is somewhat sloppy, have a strong inclination to call this *false*, or to assimilate it to the other case.

This is more likely in some cases and less so in others. One may, for example, deny that Vulcan is red without even knowing whether there is a Vulcan, just because one knows, say, that a red planet would not fulfill the conditions of the relevant astronomical theory. So either there is no such proposition as that Vulcan is red, or if there is such a proposition it is false. Anyway, there is no *true* proposition that Vulcan is red. If so, one will say in advance: 'Well, I don't know that much about Vulcan, but I know at any rate that Vulcan isn't red. I don't even know whether there is such a planet, but it is not a red one.' One might similarly say, without knowing whether there is such a kind of animal as a bandersnatch, that at any rate there are no bandersnatches in the Arctic, because one has thoroughly explored the Arctic, and one has found that nothing that could conceivably be a bandersnatch is there.

What does one mean when one says that there are no bandersnatches in the Arctic? Not that one knows that there is a proposition that there are bandersnatches in the Arctic, which one is then denying. For if it turns out that this really was a nonsense poem, there aren't just no bandersnatches in the Arctic, or even no bandersnatches at all: there is no such *kind* of animal as a bandersnatch. And we can't say: 'It happens to be true that there are no bandersnatches, though there could have been bandersnatches.' We can't say in what situation there would have been bandersnatches. Nevertheless it is natural, extending our usage, so to speak, to use 'There are no bandersnatches' to say 'There is no true proposition that there are bandersnatches (in the Arctic, or even on the whole earth).'

Similarly one might say, not knowing whether Sherlock Holmes exists or not, 'Whether or not there was a Sherlock Holmes, he isn't one of the people in this room, because the account about him was written long before any one of us had been born.' That is a conclusive enough reason. Here one should, strictly speaking, once again say 'There is no such true proposition as that Sherlock Holmes is in this room,' where I understand the purported name 'Sherlock Holmes' and can therefore refer to this alleged proposition by a 'that' clause.

What happens if one tries to apply the analysis in the case of a singular existential statement? Suppose, instead of saying 'Moses exists' or 'Sherlock Holmes exists,' or denying these, I say the following: 'There is a true proposition that Moses exists' or 'There is no true proposition that Moses exists.' Or 'There is a true proposition that Sherlock Holmes exists' or 'There is no such true proposition as that Sherlock Holmes exists.' This analysis has the peculiar feature that we know that, if there is no such *true* proposition as that Sherlock Holmes exists, we know that there is *no* such proposition, *period*; and if there *is* such a proposition (on my view) as that Moses exists, that proposition is *true*. Nevertheless, someone who hears someone else saying 'Moses exists' may well say to him—thinking to himself that Moses is a mythical entity (that is, that there is no such person as Moses)[14]: 'That is false;

---

14. But 'Moses is a mythical entity' expresses a genuine proposition. The one who believes it, however, does deny that there is a true proposition that the *person* Moses exists.

you are wrong.' In some sense he is extending the use of falsity here. It has already been extended, though, in the case of denying that there are bandersnatches in the Arctic, or that Sherlock Holmes is in this room. The man who said that Moses exists believed that he was uttering a true proposition, and, in fact, I think that he was. The man who denied it, though, did not, on my view—at least if he was a correct philosopher, which he probably wasn't— deny that proposition: rather, he thought that there was no true proposition to be enunciated.

So the tentative suggestion is this. Sometimes we use 'false' to mean that there is no true proposition of a given kind. In the case of the existential statement, if there is no true proposition, there is no such proposition at all, either. Sometimes, though, as in the case of 'There are bandersnatches in the Arctic,' we may not know which is the case. There may either be no true proposition that there are bandersnatches, or there may be such an animal as a bandersnatch, but none of them are in the Arctic, in which case the proposition in question would be false. But we lump the two cases together, and it is our ability to do so which gives the negative existential its use. The negative existential says that there is no such true proposition as that Sherlock Holmes exists—in fact, really no such proposition at all as that Sherlock Holmes exists.

Why aren't we more careful? I suppose because we are not philosophers (this is one possibility), and wish to have a convenient way of subsuming these two cases together under the same idiom, rather than saying something as complicated as my analysis. We do seem to say 'Look, there aren't any bandersnatches in the Arctic,' though it may turn out that there is no such kind of animal as a bandersnatch at all.

Another possibility is, of course, that I am wrong about this, and I do feel very tentative about this complicated and messy view. But I haven't (nor have I seen anyone else) come up with a better one. And I feel about this last problem about empty names the same as what Russell said at the end of "On Denoting"—that whatever the true theory here may be, it will not have the simplicity that one expected beforehand.

REFERENCES

Anscombe, G. E. M. (1959). *An Introduction to Wittgenstein's Tractatus*. London: Hutchinson University Library.

Austin, J. L. (1962). *Sense and Sensibilia*. Oxford: Clarendon Press.

Ayer, A. J. (1940). *The Foundations of Empirical Knowledge*. London: Macmillan.

Ayer, A. J. (1967). "Has Austin Refuted the Sense-Datum Theory?" *Synthese* 17: 117–40.

Ayer, A. J. (1969). "Rejoinder to Professor Forguson." In Fann (1969), 342–48.

Beaney, M., ed. (1997). *The Frege Reader*. Oxford: Blackwell.

Beerbohm, M. (1919). "Enoch Soames." In *Seven Men*. London: Heinemann.

Benét, S. V. (1937). "The Curfew Tolls." In *Thirteen O'Clock: Stories of Several Worlds*. New York and Toronto: Farrar & Rinehart.

Carroll, L. [C. L. Dodgson]. (1872). *Through the Looking Glass, and What Alice Found There*. London: Macmillan.

Caton, C., ed. (1963). *Philosophy and Ordinary Language*. Urbana, Ill.: University of Illinois Press.

Cartwright, R. (1960). "Negative Existentials." *Journal of Philosophy* 57: 629–39.

Chastain, C. (1975). "Reference and Context." In *Minnesota Studies in the Philosophy of Science*, edited by K. Gunderson, Vol. 7, 194–269. Minneapolis, Minn.: University of Minnesota Press.

Church, A. (1951). "The Need for Abstract Entities in Semantic Analysis." *American Academy of Arts and Sciences Proceedings* 80: 100–13.

Church, A. (1956). *Introduction to Mathematical Logic*. Princeton: Princeton University Press.

Church, A. (1995). "A Theory of the Meaning of Names." In *The Heritage of Kazimierz Ajdukiewicz*, edited by V. F. Sinisi and J. Woleski, 69–74. Amsterdam and Atlanta: Rodopi.

Davidson, D., and G. Harman, eds. (1972). *Semantics of Natural Language.* Dordrecht: Reidel.

Donnellan, K. (1966). "Reference and Definite Descriptions." *Philosophical Review* 75: 281–304.

Dummett, M. (1973). *Frege: Philosophy of Language.* London: Duckworth.

Dummett, M., G. Harman, S. Kripke, D. Lewis, B. Partee, H. Putnam, and W. V. Quine. (1974). "Second General Discussion Session." *Synthese* 27: 509–21.

Eissfeldt, O. (1935). *Molk als Opferbegriff im Punischen und Hebräischen, und das Ende des Gottes Moloch.* Halle (Saale), Germany: M. Niemeyer.

Evans, G. (1973). "The Causal Theory of Names." *Aristotelian Society Supplementary Volume* 47: 187–208. Reprinted in G. Evans, *Collected Papers.* Oxford: Clarendon Press, 1985.

Fann, K.T., ed. (1969). *Symposium on J. L. Austin.* New York: Humanities Press.

Forguson, L. W. (1969). "Has Ayer Vindicated the Sense-Datum Theory?" In Fann (1969), 309–42.

Frege, G. (1892). "Über Sinn und Bedeutung." *Zeitschrift für Philosophie und philosophische Kritik* 100: 25–50. [Translated as Frege (1997e).]

Frege, G. (1997a). "Comments on *Sinn* and *Bedeutung*." Translated by P. Long and R. White. In Beaney (1997), 172–80.

Frege, G. (1997b). "Function and Concept." Translated by P. T. Geach. In Beaney (1997), 130–48. [Originally published in 1891.]

Frege, G. (1997c). "Logic." Translated by P. Long and R. White. In Beaney (1997), 227–50.

Frege, G. (1997d). "On Concept and Object." Translated by P. T. Geach. In Beaney (1997), 181–93. [Originally published in 1892.]

Frege, G. (1997e) "On *Sinn* and *Bedeutung*." Translated by Max Black. In Beaney (1997), 151–71.

Geach, P. T. (1962). *Reference and Generality.* Ithaca, N.Y.: Cornell University Press.

Grice, H. P. (1957). "Meaning." *The Philosophical Review* 66: 377–88.

Grice, H. P. (1975) "Logic and Conversation." In *Syntax and Semantics, Volume 3: Speech Acts,* edited by P. Cole and J. Morgan, 41–58. New York: Academic Press.

Hacking, I. (1981). "Was There Ever a Radical Mistranslation?" *Analysis* 41: 171–75.

Hampshire, S. (1959). *Thought and Action.* London: Chatto and Windus.

Hintikka, J. (1962). "*Cogito, Ergo Sum*: Inference or Performance?" *Philosophical Review* 71: 3–32.

Hume, D. (1975). "Of Miracles." In *Enquiries concerning Human Understanding and concerning the Principles of Morals,* 3rd. ed., edited by L. A. Selby-Bigge, revised by P. H. Nidditch, 109–31. Oxford: Clarendon Press. [Originally published 1747.]

Kripke, S. (1959). "A Completeness Theorem in Modal Logic." *Journal of Symbolic Logic* 24: 1–14.

REFERENCES

Kripke, S. (1963). "Semantical Considerations on Modal Logic." *Acta Philosophica Fennica* 16: 83–94.

Kripke, S. (1972/1980). *Naming and Necessity*. Cambridge: Harvard University Press. [First published in Davidson and Harman (1972).]

Kripke, S. (1977). "Speaker's Reference and Semantic Reference." *Midwest Studies in Philosophy* 2: 255–76. [Reprinted in Kripke (2011a).]

Kripke, S. (1978). *Time and Identity*. Unpublished manuscript, The Saul Kripke Center.

Kripke, S. (2005). "Russell's Notion of Scope." *Mind* 114: 1005–37. [Reprinted in Kripke (2011a).]

Kripke, S. (2008). "Frege's Theory of Sense and Reference: Some Exegetical Notes." *Theoria* 74: 181–218. [Reprinted in Kripke (2011a).]

Kripke, S. (2011a). *Philosophical Troubles. Collected Papers, Volume 1*. New York, Oxford University Press.

Kripke, S. (2011b). "Vacuous Names and Fictional Entities." In Kripke (2011a).

Kripke, S. (2011c). "Unrestricted Exportation and Some Morals for the Philosophy of Language." In Kripke (2011a).

Linsky, L. (1963). "Reference and Referents." In *Philosophy and Ordinary Language*, edited by Charles Caton, 74–89. Urbana, Ill.: University of Illinois Press.

Ludlow, P., and S. Neale. (1991). "Indefinite Descriptions: In Defense of Russell." *Linguistics and Philosophy* 14: 171–202.

Moore, G. E. (1933). "Imaginary Objects." *Proceedings of the Aristotelian Society: Supplementary Volume* 12: 55–70. [Reprinted as Moore (1959a).]

Moore, G. E. (1936). "Is Existence a Predicate?" *Proceedings of the Aristotelian Society: Supplementary Volume* 15: 175–88. [Reprinted (with changes) as Moore (1959b).]

Moore, G. E. (1953). *Some Main Problems of Philosophy*. London: George Allen & Unwin.

Moore, G. E. (1959a). "Imaginary Objects." In Moore (1959c).

Moore, G. E. (1959b). "Is Existence a Predicate?" In Moore (1959c).

Moore, G. E. (1959c). *Philosophical Papers*. London: George Allen & Unwin.

Nabokov, V. (1955). *Lolita*. Paris: Olympia Press.

Neale, S. (1990). *Descriptions*. Cambridge, Mass.: MIT Press.

Ostertag, G., ed. (1998). *Definite Descriptions: A Reader*. Cambridge, Mass.: MIT Press.

Quine, W. V. O. (1940). *Mathematical Logic*. Cambridge, Mass.: Harvard University Press.

Quine, W. V. O. (1956), "Quantifiers and Propositional Attitudes." *Journal of Philosophy* 53: 177–87.

Quine, W. V. O. (1960). *Word and Object*. Cambridge, Mass.: MIT Press.

Partee, B. (1970). "Opacity, Coreference, and Pronouns." *Synthese* 21: 359–89.

Prior, A. N. (1956). "Modality and Quantification in S5." *Journal of Symbolic Logic* 21: 60–62.

Russell, B. (1905). "On Denoting." *Mind* 14: 479–93.

Russell, B. (1910–11). "Knowledge by Acquaintance and Knowledge by Description." *Proceedings of the Aristotelian Society* 11: 101–28. [Reprinted as Russell (1917a).]

Russell, B. (1912). *The Problems of Philosophy.* London: Williams and Norgate.

Russell, B. (1914). "The Relation of Sense-data to Physics." *Scientia* 4. [Reprinted as Russell (1917b).]

Russell, B. (1917a). "Knowledge by Acquaintance and Knowledge by Description." In Russell (1917c).

Russell, B. (1917b). "The Relation of Sense-data to Physics." In Russell (1917c).

Russell, B. (1917c). *Mysticism and Logic.* London: Unwin Books.

Russell, B. (1918–19). "The Philosophy of Logical Atomism." *The Monist* 28: 495–527; 29: 33–63, 190–222, 344–80. [Reprinted as Russell (1988a).]

Russell, B. (1973). *Essays in Analysis.* Edited by Douglas Lackey. London: George Allen & Unwin.

Russell, B. (1988a). "The Philosophy of Logical Atomism." In Russell (1988b).

Russell, B. (1988b). *The Collected Papers of Bertrand Russell. Volume 8: The Philosophy of Logical Atomism and Other Essays, 1914–19.* Edited by John Slater. London: Routledge.

Salmon, N. (1987). "Existence." In *Philosophical Perspectives. 1: Metaphysics,* edited by James Tomberlin, 49–108,. Atascadero, Calif.: Ridgeview.

Salmon, N. (1998). "Nonexistence." *Noûs* 32: 277–319.

Salmon, N. (2002). "Mythical Objects." In *Meaning and Truth,* edited by J. Campbell, M. O'Rourke, and D. Shier, 105–23. New York: Seven Bridges Press.

Searle, J. R. (1958). "Proper Names." *Mind* 67: 166–73.

Searle, J. R. (1979). "Referential and Attributive." *The Monist* 62: 190–208.

Spark, M. (1957). *The Comforters.* London: Macmillan.

Stalnaker, R. (1972). "Pragmatics." In Davidson and Harman (1972).

Strawson, P. (1950). "On Referring." *Mind* 59: 320–44.

Strawson, P. (1952). *Introduction to Logical Theory.* London: Methuen.

Thomasson, A. (1996). "Fiction, Modality and Dependent Abstracta." *Philosophical Studies* 84: 295–320.

Thomasson, A. (1999). *Fiction and Metaphysics.* Cambridge: Cambridge University Press.

Twain, M. (1900). *The Man That Corrupted Hadleyburg and Other Stories and Essays.* New York: Harper & Brothers.

van Inwagen, P. (1977) "Creatures of Fiction." *American Philosophical Quarterly* 14: 299–308.

van Inwagen, P. (1983). "Fiction and Metaphysics." *Philosophy and Literature* 7: 67–77.

Warnock, G. J. (1971). "On What Is Seen." In *Perception: A Philosophical Symposium,* edited by F. N. Sibley, 1–12. London: Methuen.

Warnock, G. J. (1954–55). "Seeing." *Proceedings of the Aristotelian Society* 55: 201–18.

Whately, R. (1832). *Historic Doubts relative to Napoleon Buonaparte.* Cambridge, Mass.: Brown, Shattuck.

Whitehead, A. N., and B. Russell. (1910, 1912–13/1925, 1927). *Principia Mathematica.* 3 vols. Cambridge: Cambridge University Press.

Wittgenstein, L. (1953). *Philosophical Investigations.* Translated by G. E. M. Anscombe. Oxford: Blackwell.

Wittgenstein, L. (1961) *Tractatus Logico-Philosophicus.* Translated by David Pears and Brian McGuiness. London: Routledge & Kegan Paul. [First English translation published in 1922.]

INDEX